Learning to Learn

by

S A Malone
ACMA ACIS MIIE MIITD MEd

The Chartered Institute of Management Accountants
63 Portland Place
London W1N 4AB

Throughout this book reference to the male gender implies also the female gender. No discrimination is intended.

Copyright © CIMA 1996
First published in 1994, revised 1995 by:
The Chartered Institute of Management Accountants
ISBN 1 874784 43 4

Contents

Acknowledgements

Tony Buzan is the creator of Mind Maps. The term 'Mind Maps' is the copyright of Tony Buzan.

The author would also like to acknowledge the inventor of the SQ3R Method, Professor R P Robinson.

Every attempt has been made to trace and acknowledge copyright material. The author and publisher will be happy to acknowledge copyright in future editions.

Biographical Note

Samuel Malone is an Associate of the Chartered Institute of Management Accountants, an Associate of the Institute of Chartered Secretaries and Administrators, Member of the Institute of Industrial Engineers and a Member of the Irish Institute of Training and Development. He holds a Masters degree in Education from the University of Sheffield. He is a well-known author, lecturer and training manager, and has a particular interest in mind skills.

Samuel Malone is currently employed as a lecturer in Business Management at the National College of Industrial Relations, Dublin.

Preface

*'Learning is a verb, not a noun.
It's a journey – not a destination.'*

Whether you are a full-time student, a part-time student, a correspondence course student, a practising manager who wants to improve and develop himself, or, indeed, anybody interested in developing learning-to-learn skills, this book is for you. It will show you how to organise for studying, make notes, read faster and more effectively, improve memory, maximise performance in the examination room and improve learning and problem solving skills generally.

Most people get no formal training in learning skills, and yet students with such training do consistently better in examinations than students without this knowledge. Learning-to-learn skills are not the sole preserve of students as learning is a life long process. Technology is advancing at a very rapid rate and most people will change careers a number of times in a single lifetime. As a result they will be confronted with new experiences and learning situations; for example, many managers on taking up new positions undertake informal studies and reading programmes to help them understand their new roles more adequately, while others are sent on formal off-the-job training and development courses.

The more ambitious pursue formal studies in such areas as accountancy, administration, marketing, purchasing, personnel, industrial engineering, computer science, transport and so on. Some people even undertake formal professional and university degrees in their third and fourth decades while holding down a responsible job and running a family home. Even university graduates on taking up employment often find it necessary to pursue professional qualifications and other postgraduate studies if they want to progress into middle and top management positions.

All these people need to develop learning-to-learn skills. More is now known about the brain's learning potential than ever before. Such knowledge is now available in this book and can be used to improve your learning ability. Don't rely on hearsay, old wives' tales and an unsystematic approach to learning. Apply the systematic approach outlined in this book, now!

This new edition of *Learning to Learn* has been substantially revised and expanded. New chapters on Case Studies, Tips on Presentation, Examination Stress and Examination Faults have been included while the chapters on How to Make Notes, Effective Reading and Effective Memory have been expanded.

Samuel A Malone

1
Organising Your Study

How do I plan and organise my study?
How much time should I spend studying?
Why should I use a timetable?

'The secret of success is constancy to purpose.' *Benjamin Disraeli*

Motivation

Without the proper motivation and determination to succeed, undertaking a difficult course of study such as a university degree or professional qualification can be a waste of time. Such courses require a strong commitment of time and energy and a will to succeed. If you feel you lack this commitment, most educationalists would advise you not to proceed any further. Perhaps you could use your time more productively on a less demanding programme in the same area.

'Self-confidence is the first requisite to great undertakings.' To succeed in your studies, you must be confident. The more successful you are the more confident you become in your studies and examinations. One reinforces the other.

Confidence and motivation are also interlinked. The importance of motivation cannot be overemphasised. Motivation can be derived from within oneself, such as the desire to achieve for achievement's sake. It may also be derived from external sources, such as the need for social approval, the desire for higher remuneration or the need to keep up with one's peers.

Interest in a subject also has a very strong positive motivational effect on learning and improves your capacity to learn. On the other hand, dislike for a subject has a negative motivational effect on learning. Whatever the source of your motivation, the diligent plodder often succeeds where the brilliant, but lazy, student fails. Thus, low levels of motivation can result in poor academic performance even in very able people.

Planning

The use of mnemonics, which are specially designed sets of associations, help to give organisation to otherwise unconnected material. Such mnemonic techniques include the use of rhymes, imagery and association.

They will help you in your studies, especially with remembering factual material such as terms, definitions, key points and theories. However, they are less useful where higher intellectual processes such as comprehension, application, analysis, synthesis and evaluation are involved. Nevertheless they will give you a firm foundation on which to build and develop these processes.

One such mnemonic is **PASS**. This is easy to remember for obvious reasons. **P** stands for Plan, **A** for Attention, **S** for Set Time and **S** for Systematic. Now let's look at each of these.

P*lan*. Planning is just as important to you in your studies as it is in business. Planning includes setting objectives and measuring actual performance against targets. For study purposes, just as in business, it can be conveniently subdivided into four categories. The mnemonic STOP will help you recall.

S*trategic*. Strategic plans and objectives are for up to five years ahead. Your strategic objective may be for example 'I want to become a qualified accountant in four years'. Subobjectives would be to complete each stage of the examination in one year.

T*actical*. Tactical plans and objectives cover the period for up to one year. Study the examination syllabus carefully. Ensure that your texts, study packs and correspondence school notes cover the syllabus adequately. Have a programme of studies mapped out week by week and month by month. Keep a chart monitoring your actual rate of progress against your plan. Success in keeping to your objectives will strengthen your motivation.

O*perational*. These are your day to day plans and objectives. Always set down an objective before you get down to each study session. This objective should be as concrete as possible. For instance, you may set yourself the task of memorising certain key definitions essential for success in the examination. On the other hand, you may set yourself the objective of understanding some concept in accountancy. Or you may want to get through a chapter and be able to answer satisfactorily the sample examination questions at the end.

P*rogress monitoring*. Comparing your actual progress against your objectives at each of the three levels is most important. Corrective action to remedy shortcomings should be taken to put your studies back on target again.

A*ttention*. Always focus your attention on the task at hand. Daydreaming must be eliminated if you are to succeed. When attending lectures pay attention to what is being said. Listening is a skill which improves with practice. As you listen to the lecturer try to summarise the key points in your mind, and on paper by making brief notes or using keywords. In general adopt an attitude of paying attention to detail in all things.

S*et time*. Have a set time for work and also for recreation. Time management is all important if you are to succeed in your studies. Naturally, this is going to be inconvenient and will interfere with your leisure pursuits. But if you want to succeed, you must plan your time in the form of a timetable. Also put time aside for recreation. The old saying 'all work and no play makes Jack a dull boy' should not be forgotten.

S*ystematic*. This means being methodical in your approach and working in accordance with your plan. So be systematic in all things, especially in your study. Acquire a habit and routine of studying to such an extent that, if you are not studying when you should be, you feel guilty about it.

Study time

This is often a stumbling block. How much time should you devote to study? Studying for a degree or professional qualification, especially on a part-time basis, is not an easy task. However, the task will be made more manageable if you are prepared to give it sufficient study time.

Professional accountancy examinations usually consist of four stages. As a part-time student beginning the exams, you could set yourself the objective of passing one stage each year, completing the examinations in four years. The time commitment to complete accountancy examinations in four years would need to be in the region of 16 to 20 hours per week for each stage. This assumes that you are studying on your own by correspondence course. A different profile is needed if you are attending lectures. Here 20 hours devoted to studying and attending lectures would seem reasonable. However, one can't be too dogmatic about this and you should have regard to your own particular needs.

Remember, these are just targets. Be prepared for setbacks! Most people who sit professional examinations have to repeat one or more parts. Don't let setbacks knock you off your stride. Just keep in mind that ordinary talent and extraordinary perseverance often see people through in the end. So analyse the reasons for your failure and learn from your mistakes. Be more prepared, preferably by having contingency plans, and so more resolved for your next attempt.

Of course, there can be other setbacks to your planned study programme due to events such as bereavement, sickness, change in job circumstances (current or new), domestic circumstances, or just plain lack of finance.

Analysis of study time availability

You may well be asking at this stage 'where will I get all this time for studying?' Well let's suppose that you put Saturday and Sunday aside for recreation. How much time have you available for studying? Keep a diary for a few weeks to see exactly how you spend your time. You should have at least 20 hours for study assuming you use 40 hours for sleep, 40 hours for work, 10 hours for meals and 10 hours for travelling. However, it may be necessary to devote a few hours on Saturdays coming up towards the examination for revision purposes. Remember, these are just suggestions. It may suit you better to study during the week and over weekends with mid-week breaks.

Timetables

The advantage of a timetable is that it cuts out the necessity of deciding how to allocate your time whenever you get down to do a study session. It will also help you to stick to your plan.

Basically there are two types of timetable which you should construct. Have a long-term plan for the year ahead. For day-to-day working a flexible weekly timetable is needed. In addition, a specific list of learning objectives should be written for each study session. For example, at the end of the study session you should be able to display knowledge, in writing, that you did not possess before.

Carry your timetable around with you in a notebook. Until you have decided on a firm timetable, look at it each day. Plan your studies on a daily basis and set down your learning objectives. After a few weeks experimentation compile a firm timetable.

Revise your timetable from time to time on the basis of experience, preference or social requirements. However, as time goes on it will tend to become more firm as you disengage from other commitments. You may wish to spend more time on difficult subjects or to make up for study time unavoidably lost. One last word: remember to allow time in your timetable for revision and correspondence school tests; for reflection and consolidation of information are also important.

Designing the timetable

When drawing up a timetable, take the following points into consideration.

1. Decide on the number of hours for study each week.

2. Space the hours over the week. Remember to leave at least one day per week free for recreation.

3. Decide on the time of day for study. People with jobs usually have only evenings and weekends. But even so an hour's study in the morning before leaving for work may be worth more than its equivalent at night-time because the mind may be fresher. However, if you are one of those people who never reaches peak mental performance before 11.00 am then morning study is not for you!

4. Decide how you will divide your time over the various subjects. Allocate extra time to the subjects you find most difficult or you like least. These are the very subjects that could cost you the examination. Tackle these subjects first, when you are at your freshest, rather than later.

5. Decide on the length of each study session. Psychologists have found that optimum study efficiency is maintained if the sessions are of about 45 minutes' duration, followed by a five-minute period of recall and then by a five-minute period of rest. For the latter it is a good idea to get up and walk around (out in the fresh air for a few minutes, if possible).

6. Have variety in your timetable. A change of subject will refresh the mind.

Organising and monitoring study sessions

It is said that efficient business people always start the day with a list of objectives to be achieved. Take a leaf from their book and be as specific as possible in what you plan to have achieved at the end of study sessions. Definite goals, in conjunction with your timetable, should give study sessions organisation and purpose.

After the sessions compare what you have actually learned with the learning objectives set. Knowledge of results and continuous feedback are important principles of effective learning. Monitoring your progress will ensure that you are meeting the targets of your plan. So go back and study areas you don't really know. This will ensure that you will not 'jump ahead' without knowing the material you are currently studying. Most subjects are structured on a building block basis, so premature jumping ahead will lead to confusion.

Each study session should be of about one hour's duration. Each night might consist of three study sessions each devoted to a different subject, if possible. Begin each study session with a five-minute review of the previous night's work. Finish with a five-minute review of the session's work.

Use the last five minutes of each study session for a break. Get up, stretch yourself and walk about. A good idea would be to do a few physical exercises to keep your blood flowing, such as sit-ups, tipping your toes and so on. This will keep your body supple and your mind alert.

Getting started

Getting started is often a problem Remember the saying that procrastination is the thief of time. So start actively studying straight away. Spending the first five minutes of each study session reviewing what you last studied on the subject is a way of easing yourself into the session.

When beginning to study for the first time you might find it useful to practise studying for short periods until you adapt and develop a rhythm of studying.

Concentration

Stop daydreaming the moment it starts. The first law of success is concentration and involves learning how to cope with distractions. Eliminate irrelevant thoughts, daydreams, emotions and negative feelings. Psyche yourself up to the study task at hand by saying to yourself 'Come on, now stop wasting time and get down to business'. This little technique will talk yourself back into concentration. Also, before actually studying, picture yourself effectively studying. This positive mental imagery helps create the right study mood and focuses your attention on the study task.

If you can identify a cycle of moods that you go through each week, assign the subjects you find most difficult, or like least, to the hours or day when you feel best.

Knowing you have an examination in the morning helps concentrate the mind. So imagine you are going to be examined on the content of the study session the following day. Alternatively, imagine you will be called on to give a lecture on the topic to a group of important business people.

The study environment

The place where you decide to study should be free from all noise and distractions. However, having said that, one does come across people who can study in noisy conditions. They mentally shut out the distractions. Nevertheless, noise does cause stress and therefore can never be the ideal study situation. Other people maintain that quiet background music aids rather than hinders their concentration.

You should try to study in the same place each time. You will then mentally associate a particular place with study. In fact, recent research suggests that students who sit for their examinations in the room where they study do better academically than those without this facility. This would suggest that your office, as it is naturally associated in the mind with work, might be a good place to study. Of course, using the office for part of your study (assuming your employer has no objections) has some advantages.

People with family commitments often find it very difficult to study at home because of noise and other distractions. Studying at night in the office may be a partial solution. Similarly, people living in flats or lodgings may find the office a convenient place to study.

Some organisations encourage the formation of study groups which meet on a regular basis. Members learn from each other by comparing notes, discussing difficult points and setting targets for group study sessions. The competition inherent between individuals may also motivate the less able people in the group to work a little harder.

Sit upright on a hard chair at your desk. Sitting on a sofa is not the way to study productively! The room temperature should be warm enough to make you comfortable but cold enough to keep you alert.

Noise, and other distractions, can make studying difficult.

Summary

Factors such as confidence, interest and motivation will determine to a large extent how successful you are in your examination.

The mnemonic PASS will help you remember some of the key concepts in this chapter. As you will remember PASS stands for:

1. **P**lan your studies.

2. Develop **A**ttention and concentration powers.

3. Have a **S**et time for study and leisure.

4. Work to a **S**ystem – be systematic.

    It is a good idea to work to a timetable. Study sessions should not be longer than one hour including planned breaks and review periods.

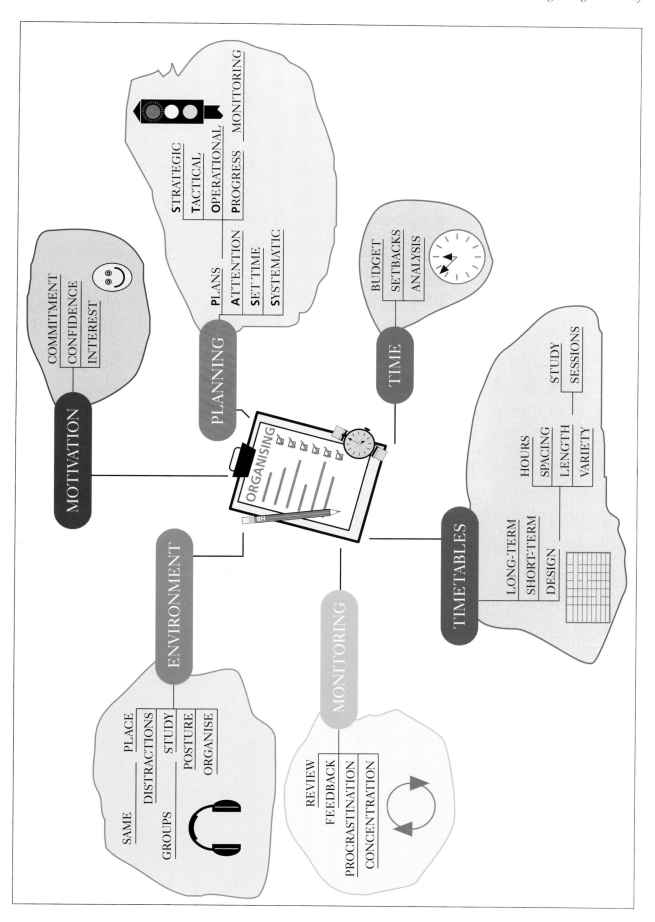

MOTIVATION
COMMITMENT
CONFIDENCE
INTEREST

PLANNING
PLANS
STRATEGIC
TACTICAL
OPERATIONAL
PROGRESS
MONITORING
ATTENTION
SET TIME
SYSTEMATIC

TIME
BUDGET
SETBACKS
ANALYSIS

ORGANISING

ENVIRONMENT
SAME
PLACE
DISTRACTIONS
GROUPS
STUDY
POSTURE
ORGANISE

MONITORING
REVIEW
FEEDBACK
PROCRASTINATION
CONCENTRATION

TIMETABLES
LONG-TERM
SHORT-TERM
DESIGN
HOURS
SPACING
LENGTH
VARIETY
STUDY
SESSIONS

2

How to Make Notes

How should I take notes?
What note-taking techniques are available?
What are Mind Maps?
How do I draw Mind Maps?
What are the advantages of Mind Maps?

'Anyone who stops learning is old, whether at twenty or eighty. Anyone who keeps learning stays young. The greatest thing in life is to keep your mind young.' *Henry Ford*

The value of notes

There are good reasons why you should take notes. First, they speed up the task of revision. It is a waste of valuable time, if every time you want to revise, you reread your textbooks or correspondence course material. If your notes are well made out, with key points and essential definitions for memorising included, it is only necessary to review the notes.

Second, the preparation of notes keeps you actively involved in your studies. The actual writing activity uses your visual and kinesthetic (i.e sensation and muscle) functions which aids concentration and reinforces the memory. This follows from the task of trying to ascertain key points and concepts for inclusion in your notes. Of course, the main advantage of notes is that they are a permanent record for revision, and coming up towards the examination are essential as a time saver.

Third, research has shown that students who take and use notes do much better in examinations than students who don't. Also review your notes periodically! For good organisation and flexibility store your notes in a loose-leaf binder. They can thus be classified and added to as your studies progress.

Fourth, note-taking is a good test of your listening, comprehension and short-term memory retention skills. In addition, notes can form the basis for discussion and study tasks with your fellow students.

Note-taking techniques

There are three basic note-taking techniques available:

1. Outline notes;
2. Detailed notes;
3. Mind Maps

Outline notes are compiled by listing trigger words which conjure up mental images of the key concepts and ideas in the main text. Outline notes are generally kept in conventional linear format. They may be transferred to pocket-sized cards which can be carried about and revised as the opportunity presents itself – for example, while commuting in a bus or train.

Detailed notes are the format used by most students. They are the student's version of the lecture. They may have been taken down verbatim or in summary form. If the lecture has been logically presented the notes may stand without further revision. However, this is not often the case, and so the notes may require editing and reorganisation. Often they need additions involving further reading, research and reflection.

Because of its shape the pattern form of note-taking is sometimes called a spider's web diagram. Another term is Mind Maps. Mind Maps are explored in detail later in this chapter.

Writing the notes

When reading a textbook or correspondence college notes don't start reading at page one and continue until the study session ends. Use the **SQ3R** method which is a mnemonic for **S**urvey, **Q**uestion, **R**ead, **R**ecall and **R**eview. We will deal with this method in detail in the next chapter. It is sufficient to say here that notes should not be taken until the **R**ecall step. If you are attending lectures, as well as doing a correspondence course, you should write up your notes and review as soon as possible after the lecture. Also, read up background material beforehand to make the lecture and note-taking more meaningful. Lecturers often fall into the trap of assuming that their audience has the same level of knowledge they have themselves.

Most textbooks are divided into chapters. The chapters in turn are divided into sections, the sections into subsections and these are then divided into paragraphs. For note-taking purposes, it is important to highlight the main ideas and definitions for memorisation. This is not as difficult a task as it seems. Most modern textbooks are well signposted and paragraphed.

The overall concept in a chapter (or correspondence college lecture) is contained in the title of the chapter. The main ideas of the chapter are in the titles of the sections. Important supporting points are in the titles of the subsections. Important details are somewhere in the paragraphs. This is the part where you must use your head. However, there are some tips. The main idea of each paragraph should be in the first sentence or last sentence. The first sentence is the topic sentence which is usually used to introduce the main point, while the last sentence either quickly summarises the content of the paragraph or introduces the point in the next paragraph. Watch out also for VERBAL and VISUAL SIGNPOSTS which will help you pick out important points.

When compiling your notes use your own words. Progressive educationalists now recommend an outline form of note-taking called Mind Maps. These may be used, depending on individual taste, in preference to the more conventional methods of linear note-taking. An example of a Mind Map is given at the end of each chapter of this book.

Mind Maps and the brain

A Mind Map is a non-linear, spatial, graphical technique where the subject matter is crystallised in a central image. The main ideas of the subject radiate from the central image as branches. Branches comprise a key image or key word printed on an associated line. Topics of lesser importance are also represented as branches attached to higher level branches. The branches form a connected nodal structure. Mind Maps may be enhanced and enriched with colour, pictures, codes, symbols and dimension to add interest. These enhancements aid memory, comprehension, motivation and the recall of information.

For example, in note-taking a Mind Map may be a visual presentation and outline of the key words of a chapter, say, in one of the student's recommended texts, distance learning units or modules. A series of micro Mind Maps can be drawn for all the chapters of a text or distance learning units. A macro Mind Map can be drawn for the entire text or for the module of a distance learning programme. One has thus an outline macro Mind Map of the entire book or module, supported by outline micro Mind Maps of each chapter or unit.

Mind Maps are just one method of diagrammatic representation of information that have been used in business and education for more than 20 years. With the advent of computer graphics, including Mind Mapping software programs, the use of such approaches is becoming more popular and accessible. Some of the diagrammatic representational systems include tables, graphs, bar charts, flow charts, organisation charts, decisions trees, Venn diagrams, algorithms and so on. All these devices incorporate abbreviated verbal information, within non-linear spatial layouts, often with colour. They differ from Mind Maps in that they have a specific use rather than a general use. For example, flow charts as used by work study practitioners or system analysts are a diagrammatic representation of a business procedure. By such methods complex systems can be grasped quickly, analysed and made more efficient. Tables and graphs are very useful for displaying statistical information. Mind Maps, on the other hand, are general-purpose models that retain the advantages of verbal and graphical representation by using words, images, symbols and colour while maintaining a great deal of flexibility.

Mind Maps simulate the structure and organisation of your brain. The average brain weighs about 3 lbs, which is about 2 per cent of the body, but takes 40 per cent to 50 per cent of the oxygen supply. It also uses 25 per cent of the calories we consume and requires many nutrients. The human brain has up to thirty billion brain cells with more than 2,000 synapses or connections between each brain cell. This gives you some idea of your learning potential. Some psychologists, such as Tony Buzan, the inventor of Mind Maps, reckon that most people use less than 1 per cent of their brain's potential. In fact to keep in top shape your brain requires love and affection, information, oxygen, and nutrition (mnemonic LION).

The brain needs proper nutrition to function. Proper amounts of protein, carbohydrates, lecithin, and vitamin B1, in particular, are needed for good brain functioning. So make sure you take a good varied diet if you want your memory to function at its best. For example, scientists have found that eating large amounts of choline, which is found abundantly in certain foods such as fish, can improve long-term memory in some people. This finding seems to support the old story that eating fish was good for your brain. The day may not be that far away when drugs will be available to improve memory function. Researchers have also found that drinking lemonade containing glucose right after studying facilitates later recall. Apparently glucose helps with the chemical processes that register long-term memories in the brain.

Your brain is organised in two halves. The two sides are connected by a large structure of 300 million neurons called the *corpus callosum*. Covering each side is a one-eighth-inch-thick, intricately folded layer of nerve cells called the cortex. Because of it, we are able to plan, organise, remember, communicate, understand, appreciate, and create: the higher intellectual skills. The left-hand side is the scientific or logic side and is into words, numbers, analysis, synthesis and evaluation. The right-hand side is the artistic or creative side and is into images, rhythm, colour and daydreaming.

Psychologists now think that although each hemisphere is dominant in certain activities the mental skills identified are now thought to be distributed throughout the cortex. Each side complements and improves the performance of the other. This integration can be encouraged and facilitated through appropriate learning experiences that require simultaneous processing from both hemispheres. Mind Maps maximise your learning effectiveness by drawing on both sides of the brain. In Western society, because of the emphasis of our educational system, our logical brain tends to be highly developed and dominant. However, our creative brain tends to be comparatively neglected. Mind Maps will help us rectify this unacceptable situation.

Making Mind Maps

Most people are unfamiliar with Mind Mapping. Because of this it is worth discussing the process in some detail and relating it to the underlying theories. The following rules are based on the Buzan method:

(a) Use an A4 sheet (or A3 sheet as needed) of blank paper. Draw the Mind Map landscape style rather than portrait style. This gives you more space to work with. The advantage of using standard 'A' sizes is obvious from the point of view of availability, photocopying, filing and so on.

(b) Start the Mind Map in the centre of the page and radiate out. This is in contrast to linear notes that start at the top left hand side of the page and work down. Draw a multi-coloured image in the centre to indicate the core and theme of the Mind Map. The Mind Map starts in the centre because this reflects the connective way that the brain thinks. This allows more space and freedom for developing ideas. Use image and colour because the old Confucian saying 'a picture speaks more than a thousand words' applies to both memory and creativity.

Psychologists have shown that images linked to words aid recall. Sketching is a most important aspect of the process because in figuring out how to draw a concept, the maker increases his understanding of it. Moving from verbalisation of an idea to a visual representation requires thinking about that idea in a new way. It means considering elements that may not have suggested themselves before, and discovering new possibilities. Therefore, making images on Mind Maps encodes the information more strongly in memory and aids recall and comprehension.

Be creative – using images on Mind Maps encodes the information more strongly in memory.

(c) Attach main themes to the central image because the brain works by association. Print words in large capital letters on top of thick lines having the same length as the words. The large capital letters and thick lines are used to emphasise the hierarchy and significance of ideas by making them more visible and thus more memorable. The linked nature of the Mind Map reflects the associative and connective nature of the brain. Some psychologists maintain that human memory is a vast, intricately interconnected network. According to such models it is not letters, syllables, or words that are recorded, but concepts and propositions. The propositions are then related in various ways to other propositions, forming an associative network. The act of encoding an event is simply forming new links and associations in the network. Mind Maps show the links and relationships between key concepts giving users an overview and a greater insight and understanding of the topic.

(d) Use a hayfork or fishbone technique to connect subsidiary lines to the main lines. These reflect the logic and associative nature of the brain. Psychologists have long established that people learn by associating new knowledge to existing knowledge and experience.

(e) Print single key words on the connecting lines (preferably one word per line). Each key word has its own range of many possible connections. Placing the key word alone on a line gives the brain more freedom to branch out in a connective fashion from that word. Phrases hide the individual word, and reduce the possibilities of further links and associations, creativity and clarity of memory. These radiant lines give the Mind Map its basic connective and associative structure. Traditional linear notes give little opportunity to add our own organisation and association. Printing on Mind Maps takes longer but it is worth the effort as it gives impact and photographic feedback to the user. Two dimensional lettering can be used to make specific key words unique and outstanding. This is in line with the Von Restorff effect in psychology which suggests that things are remembered better if they are made unusual. Making words unique and outstanding is an important feature of Mind Maps.

(f) Use colour throughout the Mind Map. Colour further enhances the Mind Map, making it more interesting, unique and outstanding and improving retention and recall. It has been found that fun and relaxation facilitates learning. This is one of the underlying assumptions of accelerated learning. So it is easier to learn new things when you are relaxed and enjoying yourself. When you are bored learning takes longer, you will tire faster, you will forget quicker and you will need to revise more often. Colour stimulates thought, creativity and memory and it appeals to the aesthetic senses. This will increase the brain's pleasure in building the Mind Map. Colour also increases interest and provides motivation to return to it for review. Psychologists maintain that colour is an important tool in visual thinking. It separates ideas, stimulates creativity, and aids memory. Colour captures and directs attention. Even linear notes can benefit from colour coding; maps, cluster maps, mandalas, and most expressive drawings are more effective in colour. When you want to highlight a key idea or point, highlighting that idea in yellow will make you, or your audience, perceive the point first. Yellow highlighters are ideal for the job of emphasising key points on the Mind Map.

(g) Ideally use images, drawings, symbols and codes throughout the Mind Map to personalise its contents to represent main themes. Tests have shown that a sharp, interactive image can improve recall of word pairs by 300 per cent compared with single rote learning. Images improve problem solving and communication and over time will improve a person's perceptual skills. Images together with colour make the content of the Mind Maps more memorable. Geniuses including Einstein and da Vinci used images in their work. For example, Einstein's ideas came to him initially as pictures and images which he subsequently translated into words and mathematical symbols. It is widely reported that he arrived at his theory of relativity while dreaming. He visualised what it would be like to travel down a sun beam. Similarly, Kekule a German chemist, discovered the molecular structure of benzene while dozing in front of the fire allowing the pattern of flames to inspire him. Extrapolating from this, the inclusion of images on Mind Maps should help retention, recall and the generation of ideas. What is noticeable about the great scientific advances throughout history is the way people combined imagination and intuition with careful reasoned analysis. It was the partnership of right and left brain that made the crucial difference. Mind Maps harmonise left and right brain thinking and enhance creativity and crystallise ideas. Unless ideas are recorded they are forgotten. Ideas externalised in a Mind Map can be explored, extended, enhanced and experimented with.

(h) Segment the main themes by drawing boundary lines around each theme. This gives the Mind Map its unique brain patterned shape. Miller, who discovered the magical number 7 plus or minus two rule in psychology, suggests that major segments should not number more than 9. Mind Maps chunk information into meaningful groups by a process of segmentation. In most practical situations there are seldom more than seven or eight subcentres, so the material in a Mind Map can be organised into a number of easily remembered chunks. Similarly, the number of chunks radiating from each subcentre again will usually be within the immediate memory capacity. Mind Maps can thus capitalise on the chunking principle by careful organisation and grouping of words within segments to maximise learning and recall.

(i) Use personalised codes and well-known abbreviations as appropriate such as 'Mgt' for management and 'Ctee' for committee etc. This saves space and speeds up processing, encoding and registration of information. Personalised codes using colours and arrows add a fourth dimension to Mind Maps. They enhance the mind mapper's ability to analyse, define, structure, organise and reason. Studies in psychology show that it is far easier for people to remember information if it is personalised. This would seem to support the use of personalised codes on Mind Maps to enhance memory.

(j) To make information more memorable invent mnemonics for key points. Use these as memory aids. Mnemonics have a long track record. Thomas Aquinas used mnemonic systems in teaching his monks. They were used by some of the kings of England and France, and by Shakespeare, Francis Bacon, and Leibnitz. Children at school use them without any prompting. Although they are still not considered totally respectable by some academics, psychologists have now established that mnemonics can indeed improve recall.

How to identify the key words

Keyword notes are far easier to recall than phrases or sentences. The brain operates on the basis of key words and images rather than sentences. The brain automatically drops the inessentials, and we should do the same in note-taking. The advantages of key words are:

1. The quantity of words is significantly reduced, facilitating faster review and revision.

2. The recorded words, if chosen appropriately, are rich in imagery.

3. The very act of extracting the key words improves concentration, understanding and the depth of processing.

Identifying the key words is an important aspect of the Mind Mapping process. The following are a few pointers which will help you to pick out the key points from a text, when drawing up Mind Map outline notes:

(a) *Hierarchy of Ideas*. When producing the Mind Map from texts use the Hierarchy of Ideas concept for choosing key words. In the case of the chapter the title should give you the main idea. Note the section titles for the main ideas of the sections. The subsections should give you the important supporting points. In other words, follow the author's organisational structure. Psychologists have found that subjects who had been shown words in hierarchies did far better in recall experiments than those who had been shown random lists. So structure and organisation as done in Mind Maps aids recall. In textbooks questions at the end of each chapter should alert you to what the author considers to be the key issues in the chapter.

(b) *Paragraphs*. It is well established that the first sentence of a paragraph is usually the topic sentence containing the main idea of the paragraph. Sometimes the key word in the topic sentence may be in italics. If so, the author has identified the main idea for you. Also, watch the last sentence of the paragraph, which may summarise quickly the key point or introduce the key point in the next paragraph. The first paragraph of a chapter may give you a quick preview of what is to come while the last paragraph may summarise what has gone before or what comes next. Similarly, the first chapter in a book may give an overview of what is to come, while the last chapter may review what has gone before. Of course, a summary at the end of a chapter, if provided, is the author's way of outlining the chapter's main ideas. Study this carefully for valuable cues as to the key points for your Mind Map.

(c) *Visual Signposts*. Visual signposts are used in a text to emphasise important points. They can be in the following formats: (1) Words in italics; (2) Words underlined; (3) Words in bold face; (4) Numbering of points; and (5) Lettering of points. Other visual signposts can be in the form of tables, graphs, pictures, diagrams, algorithms, models and charts. Some people skip over these rather than examining them closely which is worthwhile. These 'models' will clarify difficult concepts and aid comprehension and can be usefully incorporated in your Mind Map. Remember, the more images on the Mind Map, the better the recall; diagrams which use the right hemisphere and words which use the left employ both sides of the brain.

(d) *Verbal Signposts*. These are used by authors to introduce important points. For example, 'firstly... secondly' means the author is about to list details. 'On the other hand...' means the author is about to contradict a point. 'However...' means he is about to make known a qualification. 'For instance...' means he is about to introduce examples. 'Therefore...' means he is about to draw conclusions. These are useful cues to help you pick out the key words for your Mind Map.

(e) *The Pareto Principle*. In marketing, for example, this means that a small proportion of customers may account for a large proportion of the value of the business's turnover. Applied to writing it suggests that a large proportion of words are superfluous and redundant (structure words, such as 'and', 'the', 'to', etc.) and are not needed for an understanding of key concepts. The reader's job is to identify the key words. This is one of the principles on which Mind Maps are based. Sometimes people can't understand because they fail to see the wood for the trees. They avoid this by concentrating on key words and images. Mind Maps thus save considerable time when used afterwards as part of a review plan.

(f) *Recall Words.* Psychologists have long established that effective learners learn concepts and broad principles rather than cluttering their minds with detail. Thus, key words should be words that bring to mind the key concepts of the text. The more concrete they are the more memorable. Concrete words converted to visual images are on the whole more easily remembered than abstract words for which imagery is difficult. Nouns and adjectives are the easiest words to remember because they can be visualised. Thus recall words are usually nouns. They are words that trigger off other words and images. They are the hooks on which other words can be hung.

Uses of Mind Maps

You can of course use the Mind Map technique for more areas than just note-taking. For example, consider its application in the following areas:

(a) *Taking Lectures.* Use a spaced listening technique. Listen for two to three minutes, then write for half a minute. Repeat the process. Use key words only and structure the Mind Map as you go along. After the lecture restructure the Mind Map if necessary. This technique gives the listener more time to concentrate and reflect on the key issues of the lecture rather than being overwhelmed by superfluous detail. Other than by shorthand it is physically impossible to take down a lecture word for word as it is spoken. It is estimated by psychologists that speakers talk at the rate of about 135 words per minute while we can only write at about 40wpm. Therefore, trying to take notes verbatim may result in us missing most of the lecture. Mind Maps are a type of shorthand and will also help you focus on essential issues.

(b) *Giving Lectures and Public Speaking.* Why not use the Mind Map technique to prepare your talk? This will drastically cut down on your preparation time and give a natural flow to the delivery. Mind Maps enable the lecturer to maintain eye contact with the audience – a most important aspect of making effective presentations. It also provides the flexibility to stay within time. One Mind Map sheet will substitute for many cue cards or sheets that sometimes fall and get out of sequence at the worst possible time causing much embarrassment and distress. Mind Maps are imprinted on the mind during their preparation because of the concentration required to prepare them and their unique format so that recall and review is facilitated. Psychologist and author, Michael J Gelb, has written an entire book, *Present Yourself*, on the topic of public speaking based on the Mind Map approach. In fact, he uses a series of Mind Maps to summarise the content of the chapters in his book. Mind Maps may also be given out to students as advance organisers. Initially students may be confused by the unconventional layout but after a familiarisation process their response to Mind Maps is almost universally favourable. Students use them as skeletal overviews to add to and customise, if they wish, while listening to the lecture. They also use them for revision and review purposes. The more personalised students make the Mind Maps the more effective they are as learning instruments.

(c) *Writing and Reports.* Use the Mind Map technique for creating ideas and planning out your report. This will improve the clarity, conciseness, coherence, organisation, logic and sequencing of the content of your report. In a business context Mind Maps can banish writer's block from letters, reports and memos. For report writing use the Mind Map technique for planning and creating ideas. Key points can be used as headings while the supporting points can be used as subheadings. In reading complex reports use Mind Maps for review purposes and for getting a quick overview of the key issues. Mind Maps encourage creativity, gradually building up an outline as the ideas emerge. Similarly Mind Maps can be used to plan books, articles, essays, assignments and dissertations. Mind Maps are a useful way of condensing, integrating, digesting and overviewing information from many sources including research, experience, observation and reflection. Mind Maps help structure assignments in a systematic, holistic and logical fashion.

Much time can be saved using this approach.

(d) *Minutes*. What better way to quickly summarise the proceedings of a meeting than by the use of key words in a Mind Map! On a single page you can represent all the dynamics of a meeting and grasp its essence without reviewing pages of notes. The Mind Map can then be used to draw up the formal minutes. Mind Maps can be used to streamline meetings. Mind Maps improve note-taking, increases idea generating, facilitate group problem-solving and simplify communication. They increase productivity and save time.

(e) *Creativity and Brainstorming*. Why not use the Mind Map technique for creativity, problem-solving and analysis? It can be used individually or for teamwork. In business Mind Maps have been used in such areas as marketing, manufacturing, research and development, finance, strategic planning and training and development.

(f) *Study*. Students find Mind Maps very useful as a study technique in the areas of note-taking, recall and revision. They are also a useful planning aid for essays, assignments, dissertations, and answering exam questions.

Mind Map advantages

The linear method of note-taking presents many problems including deciding in what order to list facts. Where will you start? When will you end? You will have problems inserting additions and making deletions as needed. However, the biggest disadvantage of conventional presentation is that it presents a homogeneous field which is difficult to learn and get motivated about and organise in a meaningful way. A Mind Map is a *framework*; organising ideas and their advantages can be recalled by the mnemonic 'FRAMEWORK':

Flexible. Mind Maps can be developed with new and additional pieces of information by adding to the appropriate branch. With linear notes this creates organisational problems. Additions to Mind Maps may arise through serious and pastime reading, watching television, listening to radio, observation, discussion, experience and critical and reflective thought. These additions may be cross referenced to their original sources. The resultant Mind Map is a comprehensive, concentrated, conceptualised, integrated, visual and easily digestible overview and key word summary of a topic. Psychologists have found that the major circuitry of the brain is laid down by birth but the details and fine tuning continue to develop throughout life. Indeed, experience itself can cause new synapses to grow. Knowledge and experiences, then, can shape the brain. Let the Mind Map be a physical manifestation of your increased knowledge and brainpower!

Recall, *review and revise*. Rereading of textbooks, study manuals and distance learning modules is kept to a minimum. This gives you more time for revision of subjects or areas which you find most difficult. Mind Maps save time, and in preparing for professional and university degrees, especially those done on a part time basis while holding down a full time job, often with family commitments, time management is critical to success. Psychologists have shown that recall and review are essential to consolidate information in long-term memory and to optimise study effectiveness. A Mind Map with its key words, particularly if these are converted into mnemonics, is much easier to learn than twenty pages of linear notes. Also, the various mnemonics should be linked to each other or associated with existing stores of knowledge. Systematic review of Mind Maps will imprint the contents into your long-term memory.

Associations. Knowledge is in fact a pattern of connected ideas. It is the association of new information to existing stores of knowledge and experience that makes new knowledge meaningful. Therefore, Mind Maps will help to improve your memory. Meaningful learning happens when a person explicitly ties new knowledge previously learnt to relevant concepts or propositions. Relationships among concepts are more accessible in a two dimensional display than in text. Knowing how ideas are related is important for memorisation. The node-link relationship in Mind Maps helps the learner to assimilate new facts and perceive how detailed information links to the central concept. Therefore, Mind Maps by their unique brain patterned spatial structure will help you to recall trigger words and their many associations, while linking the words to each other and to the central concept.

Multi-dimensional brain. Mind Maps are analogous to the brain's own system of making connections and interconnections. Mind Maps, through an interconnective model of words and images, help people integrate both sides of their brain and contribute to whole brain learning.

Essence. The overall concept or essence highlighted at the centre of the Mind Map, with the hierarchy of ideas leading from it, provides a very clear overview. Some students fail examinations not because of insufficient work and preparation but because they clutter up their minds with detail and are thus unable to see the wood for the trees – a type of 'paralysis by analysis'. Effective study means working smarter rather than harder. It means learning concepts and broad principles rather than cluttering up the mind with details. Summarising the key points in a presentation is critical to effective learning. This final step helps students see the big picture. It helps them determine whether the pieces of information they selected were the critical pieces as they begin to read the text. In memorising anything it is vital to get an overview so that you understand the broad principles involved before you begin. A Mind Map is an overview of the key points of a text and thus aids memorisation and comprehension. When information is simply listed, it is difficult to prioritise ideas. It is also hard to see relationships, connect ideas, and see the 'big picture', and the result is a lot of information with no form of significance. The Mind Map structure graphically connects all ideas and shows the significance of each in relation to each other and to the centre.

Worthwhile visual aid. A picture is worth more than a thousand words. A Mind Map is a visual aid with impact, originality and creativity. The effectiveness of our learning is increased the more of the senses we bring into play, particularly the visual senses. Psychologists have shown that images linked to words improve recall. Hence the significance of images linked to words in Mind Maps. Why not practise mentally walking the Mind Map? With training and practice, most people can improve their capacity to use images. Visualising Mind Maps in your mind's eye will provide the training and practice and thus increase your skill at creating mental images.

Organised. Mind Maps are a structured and systematic way of getting down information and facts. Just as road maps where major roads (key concepts), minor roads (important ideas), and by-ways (important detail) can be easily differentiated by the thickness of lines, codes, dimensions, colours and so on. Psychologists have established that organisation is one of the key components of a good memory. Structure influences how incoming text information is organised. Text content for which readers have a structure is said to be better organised, elaborated and remembered. For instance, researchers have shown that a narrative about a fictitious soccer game is better recalled by readers knowledgeable about soccer than readers who have no knowledge about soccer. So background knowledge helps learning of new material, and advance organisers and structure provide the key concepts that facilitate learning and retention. Context provides a way of organising information beforehand, therefore making it more memorable. Mind Maps provide the structure, organisation and context to learn. They link new information to existing stores of knowledge in a structured framework facilitating comprehension, learning and memory.

Reconnaissance. Mind Maps will help you carry out a reconnaissance by mapping out unfamiliar terrain, particularly when used to preview chapters and complete books. Similarly, good drivers plan out unfamiliar routes by advance study of road maps. The mapping activity which Mind Maps entail imprints the information on the student's brain, making it part of his own experience and knowledge.

Knowledge of left and right brain. As already stated, the brain is divided into two separate halves. The left side or scientific brain deals with language, numbers, logic and analysis. The right side or creative brain deals with images, rhythm, colour and daydreaming. Mind Maps are an effective means of integrating both hemispheres. There is increasing evidence that the ability to put thoughts into images as well as words enhances thinking skill and actually improves intelligence. So the benefits of Mind Maps extend far beyond the practical application of recording ideas to higher order thinking and increased intelligence.

Summary

The main argument for note-taking in this context is that the students who take notes do better in examinations than those who do not. Notes should be categorised and filed neatly for reference in a loose-leaf binder.

The SQ3R method facilitates good note-taking. It is best to do the notes at the recall step. Mind Maps are recommended in preference to the more conventional method of linear note-taking. The rules of Mind Mapping are:

- Use an A4 sheet of blank paper.
- Start the Mind Map in the centre of the page and radiate out.
- Attach main themes to the central image.
- Use a hayfork or fishbone technique to connect subsidiary lines to the main lines.
- Print single key words on the connecting lines.
- Use colour throughout the Mind Map
- Ideally use images, drawings, symbols and codes throughout the Mind Map.
- Segment the main themes by drawing boundary lines around each theme.
- Use personalised codes and well-known abbreviations.
- Invent mnemonics for key points for better recall.

In addition to study, Mind Maps can be used for a wide variety of purposes including public speaking, report writing, creativity, brainstorming and problem solving.

The advantages of Mind Maps can be recalled by the mnemonic FRAMEWORK:

Flexible

Recall

Associations

Multi-dimensional brain

Essence

Worthwhile visual aid

Organised

Reconnaissance

Knowledge of brain

How to Tackle a Textbook

What is the SQ3R method?
How can it be used to improve my study skills?
How can I review for exams?

'Nothing in life is to be feared. It is only to be understood.' *Marie Curie*

Introduction – the SQ3R system

The mnemonic **SQ3R** stands for **S**urvey, **Q**uestion, **R**ead, **R**ecall and **R**eview. This method has been used successfully over the years in progressive colleges. It is a systematic method of tackling textbooks and correspondence course material. It is solidly based on psychological research and the methods of successful students. Let's now have a look at each of the SQ3R stages.

Survey

The survey stage which takes five to ten minutes is initially applied to the total book. Later you will apply the same approach to each chapter and section. This stage can be conveniently separated into three parts namely: *overview*, *preview* and *inview*. Survey is in fact a reconnaissance of the unfamiliar terrain in the book to enable you to build up reference points.

Overview

The first part of the survey stage is the overview, where you get familiar with the plan of the book. Look at the title page and cover. This should give an idea of the general subject matter, the level of person aimed at, the date of publication and the author's name, background and qualifications. Has it been written with a particular examination in mind?

The next stage is to study the preface (often called the foreword, introduction etc.) This will tell you why the author wrote the book and who was its target reader. The preface will also give you the scope and purpose of the book, its outline and structure and how to use it.

Now turn to the contents list for an overview of the topics dealt with. It will also familiarise you with the author's plan, organisation and layout. After this study the index at the back of the book. Skim down through the entries. Anything familiar or that you are already expert in? Look up the relevant section and see how the author has dealt with it. Compare this with what you know about the topic. By this technique you can judge the author's competence and knowledge of the subject and the suitability of the book for you.

Decide whether it is necessary to read the whole book or only parts relevant to your examination syllabus. You'll have time enough to read the whole book, if you're still interested, after passing your examinations. This completes the overview stage.

Preview

Preview the actual contents. Skim through the book. Read the chapter and section headings. Study with particular care any charts, diagrams, tables, pictures and graphs. The author has included these because they will illustrate some important concept where words alone would be inadequate. Bear in mind that the ability to illustrate points made in an examination answer by including diagrams, drawings or graphs wins valuable marks; for the same reason they are a substitute for word spinning.

Glance at the occasional sentences. This is the end of the preview stage.

Inview

You now apply the same approach that you applied to the book as a whole, but this time to each chapter. Carry out a detailed survey of each chapter. Study the chapter heading, section headings, subsection headings and the first and last sentence of each paragraph. Write down the two or three key concepts covered in each paragraph, but watch the relative size of headings or classification system used for clues as to the importance of ideas, organisation and structure. This completes the inview stage.

Question

This is the famous questioning technique familiar to organisation and methods or research people. It is What? Why? When? How? Where? Who? This puts you in a critical frame of mind. The following little verse by Rudyard Kipling will help you remember this questioning technique:

> *I keep six honest serving men*
> *They taught me all I knew*
> *Their names are What and Why and When*
> *and How and Where and Who*

Set down the state of your own knowledge of the subject in the form of a Mind Map. Add areas to be explored, representing gaps in your knowledge and questions to be answered.

Many textbooks have questions at the end of each chapter. Before tackling the chapter it is a good idea to look at these questions. Study the chapter with a view to answering these. The questions are in fact the author's method of highlighting important points essential to the proper understanding of the subject.

Read

Always read with a purpose. Actively seek answers to questions you have already constructed and you are likely to learn. Look for the main idea of the book, chapter, section and paragraph. This is called the *hierarchy of ideas* and is at four levels: level one the book itself, level two the chapters, level three the sections and level four the paragraphs. The Survey stage is always concerned with levels one, two and three. The Read stage is concerned with in-depth study at level four.

At the first reading don't take notes. Also, don't underline. This destroys a textbook. The best plan is to mark important sentences vertically along the margin lightly in pencil.

If you come to a stumbling block skip over it after marking it with a question mark. It may not be essential to the understanding of the rest of the chapter. In any event the material further on may explain more adequately the problem causing the stumbling block. Then go back over it and you may find that you thoroughly understand it. The worst thing you could do when you come to a stumbling block is to get discouraged and give up. The learning curve suggests that in any learning situation you will have periods of rapid progress, slow progress and no progress. Periods of slow progress and no progress are called learning plateaus. Thus there is nothing unique or unusual about your situation. It happens to all learners.

If you still don't understand the point causing the learning block, write to your correspondence school tutor or discuss it with your lecturer, with fellow students or work colleagues.

Read it again for the second time. Confirm in your own mind that you really have the main ideas at each of the levels. Pay more attention to the important details at this stage. Mark on the margin lightly in pencil the important detail which should eventually be put on your mind map.

Recall

This brings you to the recall stage. Now you should take notes by recalling what you have studied and making Mind Maps. Complete your Mind Maps by reference to the text. Some advantages of recall are as follows.

1. Recall gives you an opportunity to discover what gaps there are in your knowledge requiring remedial action. This is the learning principle of knowledge of results.

2. Recall is an active method of study rather than a passive one. By summarising your knowledge you are actively involved and getting to grips with the subject.

   How often should you recall? Mentally recall the main ideas involved at the end of each section. Recall at the end of each paragraph would disrupt the flow and continuity in reading. How much time should you spend in recalling? Approximately half your time should be spent in recalling what you've read.

   Make your notes. Use a Mind Map to record the main ideas recalled (see Chapter 2). Complete the Mind Map from the text. Reserve a column for definitions and formulae. For definitions, rules etc., recitation is the best method of memorisation.

   Remember that Recall, Recitation and Paraphrasing mentally and in writing resembles the activity in the examination room. Here you will be required to recall large areas of knowledge without the aid of notes and textbooks. You are in fact judged to a significant extent by the amount you can recall. In an examination you get no marks unless you can actually write out the required answer in the set time. It is a test of recall, comprehension, problem-solving and time management.

Review

Unless you review you forget 50 per cent of what you read immediately, and 80 per cent within 24 hours. Within a week 90 per cent will be forgotten unless reviewed, and eventually almost everything. Maintain and improve your powers of concentration by adhering to a systematic review plan. Frequent review ensures that the material in your short-term memory (STM) is transferred to your long-term memory (LTM).

Have your Mind Maps completed for the review stage. Four or five readings of textbook material may be required before its contents are familiar. If you use the Mind Maps for review these rereadings are not required. However, you should have them cross-referenced to the text. This will enable you to look up relevant points in the text when you wish to do so.

Review from the Mind Maps immediately after study, within 24 hours, after one week and again after one month. Review again after three months, and frequently coming up towards the examination. The theory behind this is that after the third or fourth review, the material under study goes into your LTM. Once this happens you need not review as frequently. Another advantage of review is that the ideas fit together more coherently. There is thus less danger of having an erroneous concept in LTM.

Review plan for examinations

In addition to using your Mind Maps for review it is a good idea to write down key ideas, difficult points or definitions on cards. Carry them around with you in your pocket for consultation during spare moments, on a bus or train for example.

Some textbooks and correspondence course material have likely examination questions at the end of each chapter. These questions cover the more important points and need particular attention.

Get past examination questions with suggested answers from the examining body. Practise answering the questions under examination conditions. Compare your attempts with the suggested answers. Make sure that if given the opportunity again you would get 100 per cent of the marks. Some examination topics come up time and time again.

Submit the relevant tests to your tutor or correspondence college on the due date. When you get them back study the examiner's comments. This is important feedback. Learn from your mistakes and ensure that you won't repeat them again.

And finally, get past examiners' reports from your examining body. These give you important tips as regards pitfalls to be avoided and weaknesses generally experienced by students.

Write down key ideas and difficult points on cards. Carry them around with you.

Summary

The SQ3R method is recommended as a systematic approach to studying most written material. You may remember that SQ3R stands for:

- **S**urvey. This in turn was further subdivided into *overview*, *preview* and *inview* stages. Study the preface, contents list, index, layout, chapter summaries and so on.

- **Q**uestion. Pose questions to yourself that you want answered. Such questions may be prompted by studying the questions, if any, at the end of the chapter.

- **R**ead. Read with a purpose, actively in search of answers and ideas.

- **R**ecall. Try to recall the gist of what you have read at the end of each section and take notes at this stage, preferably in the form of Mind Maps.

- **R**eview. Use your Mind Maps to review and revise what you have learned.

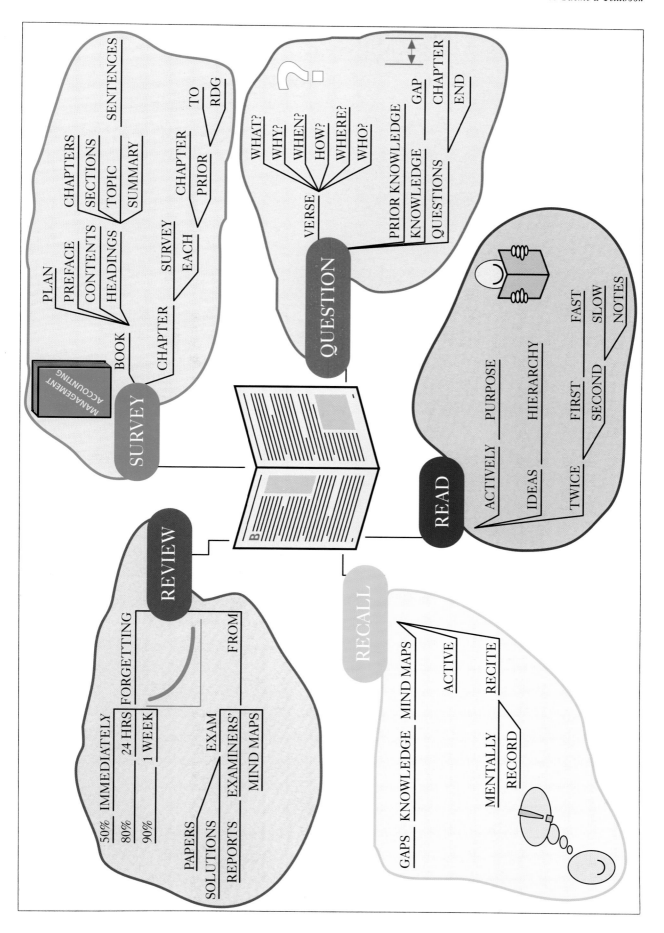

Effective Reading

What are the barriers to effective reading?
How are visual and verbal signposts used to emphasise important points?
How can I improve my concentration?
How can I improve my reading skills?
What are the goal focused approaches to reading?

'Reading is to the mind what exercise is to the body.' *Sir Richard Steele*

Better reading

Before you can become a more effective reader you should know some of the barriers to meaningful reading. A lack of understanding of written matter may not be your fault. It may be because of the author's poor presentation.

When buying textbooks make sure they meet some of the following criteria. They should be well laid out with clear signposting, free from ambiguity, indexed, easy to read and understand, cover the syllabus and include a glossary. Most important of all, you should feel comfortable with your textbook. In practice you may have to look around for some time before you find a book that meets your particular needs.

For better reading use the SQ3R method. This technique will help you to anticipate information and discriminate as to what is important to your purpose, what is less important and what is irrelevant.

Apply the questioning approach

When reading, adopt a 'doubting Thomas' approach. Evaluate the text in a critical and questioning way. Keep the following questions in the forefront of your mind:

1. Are his facts correct? In most reputable textbooks they probably are.

2. Does the author distinguish between facts, assumptions and opinions?

3. Are conclusions developed logically from the facts?

4. What other conclusions could be drawn?

5. Do you agree with the conclusions reached?

6. Are there contrary viewpoints?

7. Are some of the claims made unproved, or can they be supported by empirical research?

This questioning technique will make your reading more active and purposeful with a greater understanding and retention of the material read. Watch out for limitations, exceptions, contradictions, arguments against any statement made, similarities and differences between theories discussed.

Relate the text to your own experience and more generally to your working environment. In most companies you have departments dealing with the areas you will meet in your studies e.g. accountancy, auditing, management services, finance, marketing, law, personnel, office administration, management accounting and purchasing and supply. Find out what is happening in these areas in your firm and relate them to your studies. You will soon begin to realise that your theoretical studies have a down to earth practical application.

Faster reading

It has now been established that with training you can read considerably faster without any loss of comprehension. The average reader reads at a speed of 240 words per minute. This can be improved, with a little training, to a speed of 360wpm. With sustained effort and plenty of practice you can achieve 600wpm when reading easy material. For more difficult material, and in order to maintain comprehension levels, you should be satisfied with a reading rate of 400wpm. On the other hand, according to research studies, there appears to be a minimal reading speed of 200wpm below which the reader may fail to process the meaning of text effectively.

Reading below 200wpm apparently reflects inefficient, word-by-word reading which is not conducive to integrating and comprehending text in a meaningful way. Research has also shown that when the term reading is interpreted in the sense of comprehending most of the words on a page, it is impossible to read faster than 800 to 1,000wpm and that comprehension suffers significantly above a speed of 400wpm. The capacity of the working memory is also a constraint. Of course, higher speeds can be achieved when approaches such as skimming, scanning and skipping are employed but this should be distinguished from genuine reading.

Research has shown that the eyes move with a jerky, intermittent motion. The brain reads words at each fixation. This means you can read only when your eyes momentarily stop; each stop is called a fixation. To be a faster reader, therefore, you must increase your *recognition span*. The recognition or perceptual span is about three words. Reading for ideas by chunking words means that you will have fewer fixations, taking in larger groups of words with a faster reading speed.

In general it has been found that ineffective readers suffer from the following defects.

1. They have small recognition spans. They read each word individually. This makes the flow of their reading disjointed and hinders comprehension. Try to read a whole phrase instantaneously.

2. They make regressions. Their eyes drift back to reread words and phrases. This shows a lack of confidence in their reading ability as more than likely they have absorbed what they have read. This habit destroys concentration. Making regressions may also be caused by your eyes losing their place on the page.

3. They vocalise. This is a hangover from schooldays and as a result speed and quality of reading suffer. However, in certain circumstances, such as revision, vocalising can aid memory. Most readers subvocalise i.e. say words internally to themselves. You can speed up your reading by not subvocalising structure words, such as 'and', 'the' etc. However, subvocalising key words has been proved by psychologists to aid memory.

4. Because ineffective readers have small recognition spans, they make many eye fixations which in turn slows down reading.

5. Ineffective readers do not vary their reading speed in line with their purpose, level of knowledge and the difficulty of the reading matter. The good reader sees more in less time and varies reading rate in line with their purpose and the difficulty of the text.

6. Ineffective readers fail to integrate prior knowledge and experience with text information and do not apply critical reading skills such as analysis, synthesis and evaluation to the written text.

7. Ineffective readers may have a small working memory capacity and consequently have less capacity for maintaining previous information and integrating new information. On the other

hand, good readers with a large working memory should be able to retain more of a text in working memory while processing new text, so their integration of the information may be more thorough.

Reading techniques

Use to your benefit the difference between rapid reading, skipping, skimming, scanning and reading slowly. Skimming is where your eyes cover certain preselected sections of the text to gain a general overview. Scanning is where your eyes glance over material to find a particular piece of information. You could employ rapid or fast reading to advantage when dealing with a novel or a not too difficult text. Obviously, with light material you can follow the story line without reading every word carefully. If you are reading for specific information, as in research, you should skip reading matter not essential to your purpose. The index can be used to advantage here.

To survey a book employ the skimming technique described earlier.

Finally, with difficult texts you must read slowly for comprehension. The latter is the type of reading normally suitable for studying. But remember, vary your style of reading in line with the purpose. Read quickly material that you are already familiar with. Read slowly material that is new to you or that you find difficult.

With difficult texts you may have to read more slowly.

Seven ways to improve your reading skills

These can be brought to mind by the mnemonic 'VERTIGO' as follows:

Vocabulary. Being unable to recognise the meaning of words will slow you up considerably, although context and inference can provide clues as to meaning. You can read better if you know more words. So build up your vocabulary. To do this you must:

1. Read widely. The more knowledge you have the easier it is to acquire more knowledge.

2. Study common prefixes and suffixes. A prefix is one or more syllables added at the beginning of a word to qualify its meaning while a suffix is added at the end. For example, in the word 'premeditated' the 'pre' which means 'before' is the prefix, meditate means to think, and the 'ed' is the suffix which refers to the past tense. Word analysis or breaking a word into its component parts, as above, is a useful strategy to adopt for understanding words without referring to a dictionary.

3. Watch out for new words. Record these on cue cards for reference. File these alphabetically and review periodically. Alternatively carry them with you and review during spare moments of the day. As you commit the words to long-term memory destroy the cards.

4. Use the new words you learn at every available opportunity. Integrate them into your normal everyday conversation and thereby commit them to long-term memory.

5. Compile a glossary of technical terms in your subject or better still, if available, get one of the specialist dictionaries in your chosen field. Use this approach to build up your technical vocabulary in your specialist subjects.

Eyesight. If your eyesight is bad and affecting your ability to read, then get a pair of spectacles. Amazingly, many people neglect this because of vanity or inertia. During reading sessions take a rest occasionally and focus your eyes on a distant object. This will relax and rest the eyes and prevent fatigue.

Regression. Stop regressing. Don't go back over words you think you don't understand. More often than not the meaning will become clear because of context and structure as you continue reading.

Talking. If you find yourself vocalising, stop talking to yourself! However, there is one exception to this. When revising it is often a good idea to speak the key material aloud for better impact and retention. Reduce the amount of subvocalising and speed up your reading by avoiding subvocalising structure words. In fact, the faster you read the less subvocalising you will be capable of doing.

Ideas. Read in thought (idea or concept) units. Increase your recognition span. For example, when next reading the newspaper fix your eyes on the centre of each sentence of a column. With practice your eyes should be able to take in the beginning and end of the sentence automatically. The columnar structure of newspapers facilitates this process. When reading a text, chunk words in groups of two or three at a time which is the size of the perceptual span. Good readers attend primarily to the meaning of the text while poor readers attend more to its surface characteristics.

Guide. Use a visual guide such as your index finger, a pencil or pen. Run it along under the line you are reading without touching the page. Vary your speed in line with your purpose and the difficulty of the text as you go along. This technique focuses your attention on what you are doing and thereby improves your concentration. You won't regress through losing your place on the page. Using the hand as a pacer allows you to see and read groups of words at a time and helps to reduce subvocalisation. It adds rhythm to reading, which involves the right side of the brain. Also, two senses are involved, the sense of vision and the sense of touch, thus increasing your command. Readers may also lose time through slow recovery time. This is the time it takes to move from one line to the next. Consciously speed up your index finger when going from one line to the next to minimise the recovery time and speed up your reading. Always maintain an upright but relaxed posture. The desk you are reading at should be at a suitable height. Some experts maintain that the distance between your eyes and the book should be between 15 and 24 inches. Obviously using a guide is only appropriate for serious reading rather than leisure reading where the emphasis is on relaxation and enjoyment.

Operating reading speed. Determine your existing speed. If this is average or below there is no reason why you can't improve it by between 50 per cent and 100 per cent without loss of comprehension. So practise reading faster. This should be done straightaway! The editorials in the newspaper each morning can be used for practice sessions. More importantly apply the rapid reading technique to your study material as appropriate. Compete with yourself. Make each reading a step towards more effective reading.

It's a good approach to improving your reading skills if you work on one idea at a time. When you are satisfied that you are proficient in that aspect then move on to the next idea. By this process you will build up your skills on a gradual but permanent basis. Also, for more effective and permanent learning distribute your practice over a period of time.

Improved concentration

Your concentration is an essential ingredient for successful reading. Without good concentration you will not retain and learn what you have read. Find a quiet place to read free from noise, distractions and interruptions. Classical music, such as the baroque music of Bach and Handel, played in the background while reading can induce relaxation, make the mind alert and improve concentration. The mnemonic 'DISPOSAL' will help you remember the main points for developing powers of good concentration.

D*ivide and conquer*. Adopt a psychological attitude of divide and conquer. Instead of reading a book, read chapters. Instead of reading chapters, read sections and paragraphs. This chunking has the psychological effect of making the task more manageable.

I*nstead of problems focus on benefits*. The perceived benefits must outweigh the difficulties. What benefits will accrue to you as a result of reading the book? This will create interest and motivation to read the text.

S*tart and finish time*. Estimate how long it should take to read. Have a time block for each reading session with a start time and estimated finish time – 'That which can be done at any time, rarely gets done at all'. So apply time management techniques to your reading tasks.,Refer back to Chapter 1 for tips on how to do this.

P*ositive self-talk*. Attitude is an important aspect of good concentration. We are what we think we are. If you think you can you will. If you think you can't you won't. You set your own psychological limits. To improve your concentration say to yourself, 'My concentration is very focused. I am totally concentrated.' Feed this into your subconscious over a period of time so that it becomes part of your mental set. Impaired concentration can be caused by a conflict between will and imagination. We must develop positive and constructive use of the imagination to help focus our powers of concentration. Relax and use repetition each day to imprint affirmations and images into your subconscious.

O*ngoing recall*. Spend up to 50 per cent of your time recalling. Take notes, preferably in Mind Map form, at the recall stage and use these for review. Adopt the 5 R approach: Read, Recall, Review, Relax and Reflect. Generate images for key words as visual memory lasts longer than verbal memory. With models, diagrams and pictures use your powers of visual imagination. Try to visualise the diagram or picture in your mind's eye. With practice you should get better at this. These exercises bring the right or imaginative side of the brain into play. Using both sides of your brain will enhance your learning effectiveness. Relax using a deep breathing exercise or progressive muscle relaxation. For the deep breathing exercise sit comfortably with your arms at your sides. Using your diaphragm, inhale slowly through your nose to a count of four. Hold your breath to a count of four. Exhale through your mouth to a count of four. Rest for a count of four. Repeat the exercise a few times. For the progressive muscle exercise sit comfortably with your arms at your sides. Take a few deep breaths as above. Starting with your feet, visualise a warm orange glow relaxing every muscle in your body as it slowly moves its way up, ending with the muscles in your face.

S*pecific objectives*. Read with a purpose. Specify your learning objectives at the outset and self-test at the end of the reading session. Reading with specific objectives in mind directs attention and facilitates comprehension of relevant information.

A*ttend to task*. Procrastination is the thief of time. Procrastination has been defined as the automatic postponement of an unpleasant task, for no good reason. So start it now! Do it now! Take a point of view or perspective as you read to enhance your recall. Naturally, in your own case this will be the point of view of a person who wants to improve their reading skills. Ask yourself, how will the application of these ideas improve my reading skills?

Look *for interest*. Attention, interest and motivation are interlinked. To improve your attention you must eliminate external and internal distractions. To eliminate external distractions create a proper work environment, read in a quiet place or with baroque background music, organise your work space, use good lighting and sit in a comfortable chair. To eliminate internal distractions relax, know your biorhythms and plan your reading accordingly, verbalise and visualise what you want, set specific realistic goals and break your goals into manageable subgoals. Interest creates motivation. Relate what you read to your own experience and existing knowledge. Whenever possible, choose areas in which you have a natural interest. People learn by linking and associating new knowledge to what they know already. The effective reader quickly integrates prior knowledge and experience with text information.

Reading approaches

When reading vary your reading speed with your purpose. For example, the following types of goal reading approaches should be noted and used as appropriate. Use the mnemonic 'SCRIBE' to help you recall the methods involved.

Specific. You may read to research a topic of interest to you or to get specific information for example for a particular problem or exam question you want to solve. Use the index at the back of the book to guide you to the particular section that interests you; then read this section carefully. This is an example of reading with a purpose.

Critical. Critical reading involves making inferences, assumptions, deductions, interpretations, predictions and evaluations. Critical reading is essential for study. You must learn to discriminate between what is important and what is not. Is it relevant or irrelevant? Is it supported by the argument or not? Apply the higher level thinking skills such as analysis, synthesis and evaluation to the written text. To support your critical reading approach apply a creative reading strategy. Creative reading involves synthesis, integration, application and extension of ideas. It means making the reading your own and getting more out of it than is actually there.

Revision. Revision reading is done to confirm knowledge and help retain it in your long-term memory. Use the Mind Maps for this purpose, and be thoroughly familiar with all the main concepts. Skipping and skimming can be used with advantage here especially when reading texts.

Informational. Additional reading is essential for most subjects to give you familiarity and a broad background knowledge. Reading around your subject will give you different perspectives and a greater insight and understanding of the topic. However, do refer to your syllabus so that you concentrate on those aspects which are topical and relevant.

Browsing. Lunch-time often presents opportunities to visit a bookshop or library to browse. Browsing can be an educational, relaxing and rewarding pastime and can form an integral part of your effective study time management system. Take the opportunity to browse through texts which do not seem wholly relevant to your syllabus. Practise your skipping and skimming techniques as appropriate, critically reading only those sections which are of importance to you.

Enjoyment. Of course, we all read for relaxation and enjoyment. As you know when reading a novel it is not necessary to read every single word to get the gist of the story. Apply rapid reading techniques here, scanning, skipping and skimming as necessary.

Proofreading is an approach which is not obviously applicable to a student's needs. However, a variation on the theme, such as review or check reading, should be your approach on completing an answer in the examination. Checkread for grammar, punctuation, misspellings, sense and neatness. Is (A) always followed by (B) and have you demonstrated it? At work the same approach can be applied to letters or reports prepared by you. In practice this simple procedure is often overlooked.

Summary

For better reading use the **SQ3R** method: **S**urvey, **Q**uestion, **R**ead, **R**ecall and **R**eview. Some barriers to effective reading were highlighted. The average person has a reading speed of 240 words per minute. By efficient reading methods this speed can be improved to about 360wpm with an upper limit of 600wpm for conventional reading.

There are seven main ways in which you can improve your reading skills. These can be recalled by the mnemonic 'VERTIGO' as follows.

Vocabulary. Improve your vocabulary.

Eyesight. Wear spectacles if you need them.

Regression. Stop going back over words.

Talking. Stop talking to yourself and reduce subvocalising or inner speech.

Ideas. Read for main ideas. Grasp them in thought units and increase your recognition span.

Guide. Use a visual guide such as your index finger.

Operating reading speed. Practise reading faster. Use skipping and skimming techniques as appropriate.

Good concentration makes a key contribution to effective reading skills. The mnemonic 'DISPOSAL' will help you to remember the main points for developing powers of good concentration:

Divide and conquer.

Instead of problems focus on benefits.

Start and finish times.

Positive self-talk.

Ongoing recall.

Specific objectives.

Attend to task.

Look for interest.

Reading with a purpose is an important aspect of effective reading. The mnemonic 'SCRIBE' will help you to recall the methods involved:

Specific.

Critical.

Revision.

Informational.

Browsing.

Enjoyment.

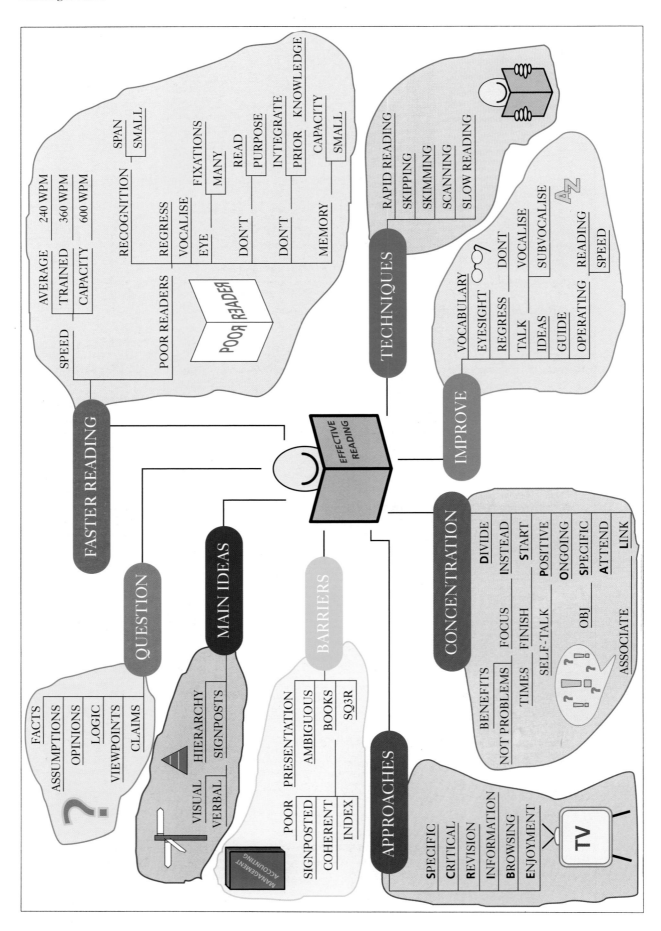

Effective Memory

What are the laws of remembering?
How can I improve my memory?
What is the PLAN system of memory?
How can I use mnemonics to improve my recall?
What is the systematic approach to applying memory to exam topics?

'A man's real possession is his memory. In nothing else is he rich, in nothing else is he poor.'
Alexander Smith.

General principles

The average person uses only 10 per cent of his normal memory capacity. In case this 'regularly' quoted statistic is not thought-provoking enough, it is now felt that you are not using even 1 per cent of your brain's potential. There is obviously plenty of room for improvement! Memory is a very important study skill. To pass examinations you need to build up an adequate database of knowledge for each of the subjects on your syllabus. Most people know very little about how their memory works. Very few people get any training on memory techniques which can enhance their ability to recall information. In this chapter I hope to give you a few practical tips that will help you remember things better, especially in the area that concerns you most – study! Throughout this chapter I will be using mnemonics as vehicles for organising key points on memory and also to illustrate how these devices can be used to help you recall information instantly. A knowledge of the laws of memory and, of course, use of that knowledge can help you utilise some of the spare capacity of your brain. Let's now discuss the three laws of memory and our first mnemonic – **I**mpression, **R**epetition, and **A**ssociation (IRA).

Impression

Get a deep vivid impression of what you want to remember. To do this you must concentrate and focus your attention on the material you are studying. Use your powers of observation. A camera won't take good pictures in poor lighting conditions. Similarly, your mind won't register and remember impressions when there are inconsistencies in your mental ideas of a subject.

Impression is therefore the ability to imagine or picture what you want to remember in your mind's eye. Reading is a left brain function. This is the side of the brain which specialises in logic, words, numbers and language. To make your reading more memorable you also need to use the right hand side of the brain which specialises in creativity, imagination, colour and daydreaming. So when you're reading try to live and visualise the experience. At first you may find this difficult to do. Nevertheless, the very fact that you are trying will improve your concentration and thus help you remember information better.

External impressions such as sight, sound, smell, touch and taste are got by keeping your eyes open, observing and actively getting involved in the world about you. Internal impressions such as interest, understanding and attention are got by closing your eyes, visualising and reflecting on your experience. For example, when trying to recall a section of a book you could try to visualise the key points in your mind's eye or better still write them down.

Employ all your different senses. Visual for pages, diagrams and pictures. Auditory for paraphrasing, recitation and reading aloud. The sense of touch and imagination for note-taking and visualisation. Forming mental images or drawing diagrams or flow charts of key study material will help you to understand it. Drawing or note-taking uses the left or verbal side of the brain. Using imagination draws on the right or visual side of your brain. Thus your ability to recall the information is more than doubled.

Forming mental images or drawing diagrams or flowcharts about study topics will help you to understand and to imprint the information on your mind. Some educationalists argue that this is effective because it involves the left (logic) and right (creative) hemispheres of the brain. On the other hand, drawing diagrams or flow charts brings the right or creative side of the brain into action. Thus your chances of understanding and recalling the information are multiplied.

Live the experiences by visualising the use of as many of the senses as possible. For example, when studying Company Law picture the process involved when registering a limited company. Imagine yourself completing the necessary documentation. Sense the feel of the paper. Picture the inside of Companies House and the bureaucratic hassle you might go through to get the registration finalised. To make the process stand out in your mind even more, imagine you have a ferocious argument with the official at Companies House about some aspect of the procedure.

Discuss the lecture or chapter with a fellow student after reading it. The discussion will give you different perspectives on the topic while holding your concentration and stimulating your mind. It also brings variety into the study approach. Set up formal study sessions groups to discuss course related topics. Set aside one or two hours say each Saturday morning for this purpose.

Develop an interest in your topic for better learning and recall. Read around your topic. At the very least read an appropriate professional journal and the business pages in the newspapers. Interest creates motivation and counteracts boredom. Integrate what you want to remember into your everyday activities. Information is forgotten quickly if not actively used.

If you dramatise, personalise and emotionalise something you are more likely to remember it. Therefore put **M**ovement, **U**nusualness, **S**lapstick and **E**xaggeration into your mental images. So remember the mnemonic MUSE (in mythology a Muse was one of the nine goddesses inspiring learning and the arts) for more effective recall.

Study material is retained better if it answers a question. Put down in a Mind Map the amount of knowledge that you already have on the topic and the answers to the questions that you seek. This is the knowledge gap. This exercise creates the proper mental set or attitude for study.

The three Rs of memory are **R**eception, **R**etention and **R**ecall. GIGO is a well known mnemonic used in computer circles. GIGO stands for 'garbage in, garbage out'. The same idea can be used in learning and memory. Obviously, to remember something you've got to register it on your imagination. Constantly reflecting and thinking about your subject will ensure this process takes place. This will ensure that the information is retained in your long-term memory. What you are doing, of course, is overlearning the information. Recall is the ability to be able to reproduce the material in writing inside the exam room without the support of books for reference. When recalling use your vivid imagination. Written words in themselves are dead. The author had pictures in his head before actually writing the words and you must translate the words back into pictures.

Repetition

The second law of memory is repetition. Muslim students memorise the Koran – a book as long as the New Testament – by repetition. Repetition is how we learnt the times tables at school and also how we learnt the alphabet. Psychologists call this overlearning. The material has been embedded in our long-term memory. This is the approach you need to adopt when learning key points and important definitions. I would not recommend rote learning except in this particular instance. Build up your database of key points and concepts in your topic and you can expand on these yourself. When using the repetition technique keep the following points in mind.

Space out your repetition for better recall. Go over it a few times, then drop it; come back later and go over it again. Reviewing at intervals in this manner will help you memorise in about half the time it takes to do so at one sitting. Keep a review file. Imagine you take some notes on 1 January. Do review 1 on 1 January. Date your notes for the second review. In this case it will be on 2 January i.e. 24 hours later. Therefore, put 2 January on the top of your notes. Review 3 will be on 9 January. Review 4 will be on 4 February. Review 5 will be on 4 June. This will anchor the key points into your long-term memory. Each day check the date on each page of your notes. Notes with today's date on them should be reviewed now and then forward dated for the next review. In general, review from Mind Maps, cue cards, review questions at the end of chapters, past exam questions and answers, lecturer's comments and examiner's reports.

Discuss the chapter with a colleague after reading it and thereby reinforce the memory of it. When reading imagine that you will be called on to give a lecture on the topic.

This has the marvellous effect of focusing the mind on the topic. On a lower key, imagine that you will be required to explain it to a friend after reading it.

Alternate periods of reading and recall. Recall at the end of each section and again at the end of each chapter. Paraphrase the author's thoughts in your own words. Recalling constantly aids reading comprehension and monitors progress. The first time you do this write down the points you can recall. Compare these with the text and fill in the gaps. Use these notes to compile your Mind Maps of key points. In a typical study session spend 50 per cent of your time recalling. Continuous feedback through recall is essential for effective memory.

Think about your subject during spare moments of the day. Use cue cards for this purpose. For example, walking along the street, waiting for a bus or commuting to and from work. The famous American psychologist William James said 'the one who thinks over his experiences most and weaves them into systematic relations with each other will be the one with the best memory'.

In recalling information, don't just verbalise the recall, write it down. Better still, do a Mind Map of the key points. This is a left-brain activity. To make it more memorable, reflect on the topic and actively associate information to make it unique and outstanding. Picture the information in your mind's eye. This process draws on the right side of your brain.

Association

The third law of memory is association. Association means linking study material with information and experience that you already know. Relate your professional studies to your work and try to integrate them with your everyday life experience. Apply the questioning technique to build up the necessary links and to engrave the subject matter on your memory. Why is this so? How is this so? When is it so? Where is it so? Who said it? What else could be deduced? The more the brain is used, the more memory associations are formed. The more associations are formed, the easier it is to remember previously acquired information, and also to form new associations.

There are three laws of association which you may find useful to know. The first law is called the law of similarity. This states that two ideas may be associated if they resemble each other. For example, people with the same name. The second law of association is called the law of contrast. This states that two ideas may be associated if they contrast with each other. For example, tall and short, day and night. These laws suggests that comparing and contrasting ideas is a very effective way of learning information. The third law is called the law of contiguity. This states that two ideas may be associated if they have occurred together. For example, if two important events happened on similar or near enough dates one may be recalled by reference to the other. We all know that the First World War started in 1914. Frederick Winslow Taylor, the 'father of scientific management', died the following year in 1915. Connect the two events and you now have a way of recalling the date of Taylor's death.

Information is retained better if obtained in answer to a question. This creates active learning and the proper mental set. Put down in Mind Map form the knowledge you have already about the topic and the questions that you want answered. Develop an interest in the subject as this will improve your ability to learn and recall. Integrate what you want to remember into everyday activities. Things are forgotten through disuse.

People tend to have better recall of items which are linked, categorised and conceptually related in some way. Mind Maps will help you to do this. Short-term memory (STM) is the amount of information a person can recognise and recall after a single presentation without practice. STM decays rapidly without rehearsal, with estimates ranging up to 18 seconds duration. Like long-term memory, interference seems to be the prime cause of forgetting in STM.

The capacity of STM is between five and nine items of information. However, its capacity can be extended if the material is grouped. For example, a memory span of seven letters can be increased to 35 if the letters form seven five letter words. Therefore, 'chunk' the learning points into related groups of between five and nine items. Thus isolated words such as mnemonics can be easily memorised if you are astute enough to organise them into a meaningful sentence or a little story. Whole areas of a topic can therefore be recalled quite easily. In memorising, say, a definition, the central part requires more attention than the two extremes. So make the central part unique and outstanding and you will remember it better.

Use the SQ3R method described earlier. The survey, question part of this formula gives you the framework and hooks to associate information to as you read.

Information that is organised can be learnt much faster than information which is not. Reading strategies that pay attention to individual ideas, and to how they are organised and related, produce better recall. There are three techniques for mental organisation. First, there is sequencing which means putting items into chronological or alphabetical order. Second, there is categorising which means grouping items according to some common characteristic such as colour, shape or other similarity. Third, there is relational imagery which means organising items round a theme such as work, holidays, Christmas etc. People remember things better in relation to a particular context. Contextual features become associated with material being learned, and can serve as cues for recall.

Memory and understanding

Let's now look at the 'MUD' principle. MUD is a mnemonic standing for **M**emory, **U**nderstanding and **D**oing. Obviously, if you really want to remember something you should understand it. Memory is but one of the ingredients of effective learning. Memorising involves association, repetition, review, paraphrasing and self-testing. Understanding involves questioning, comparing, contrasting, analysis, synthesis and problem solving. Doing involves a physical activity of some sort with practice sessions to achieve perfection. Professional and university examinations test students' capacity to demonstrate their analytical and problem solving abilities rather than mere rote memorisation. Therefore, organise your material, be thorough and make sure that you understand what you are committing to memory.

The greater our existing knowledge, the greater our insight, understanding and ability to make meaningful associations. Wide and extensive reading will provide a sound foundation on which additional knowledge can be built. Pay attention to meanings and make extensive use of associations. Look for similarities, contrasts, advantages and disadvantages and relate everything you can to your fund of knowledge and experience. Use the SQ3R system for better understanding, retention and recall.

Detailed memory laws – FIBRES

Brain cells when viewed under a microscope look like tiny octopuses with tentacles or fibres emanating from them. This should help you link the mnemonic FIBRES with memory. FIBRES is really an elaboration of the three basic laws I discussed in the previous few paragraphs. FIBRES stands for **F**requency, **I**ntensity, **B**elonging, **R**ecency, **E**ffect (Pygmalion) and **S**tand out (unique and outstanding). Let's now look at each of these laws!

Frequency. This means exactly the same as repetition. The more often one learns the better one knows it. Overlearn so that in the examination room you won't have difficulty recalling information, even if under stress. The best way to commit a passage to memory is by the 'progressive part method'. In this method the learner adds a new line while continuing to rehearse the other lines. For example, if you learn line one you would then learn lines one and two. When you have these memorised you would then tackle lines one, two and three, and so on. Such a procedure ensures:

1. that our short-term memory is not overloaded;

2. the practice and retention of earlier lines, otherwise forgotten through interference.

For best results, the 'progressive part method' should be combined with the 'holistic method' (see below). In other words, get an overview of the material first before using the progressive part method. This is the concept behind the SQ3R system. Build up a framework of the area to be studied and then develop this as your studies progress.

Intensity. Intensity, motivation, interest and confidence are all interlinked. Each reinforces the other. The more success you have, the more confident and motivated you become. Similarly, the more enthusiastic you are about a topic the better your recall. For example, a schoolboy may be thought to be stupid and indifferent at studies and yet may have an amazing capacity to recall all the players in his favourite football team, what matches they won and even who scored the vital goals. The reason for this, of course, is that soccer has caught his imagination and interest. In reality it is hard to have an intense interest in all the topics that you study, nevertheless be aware of this factor and try to build up enthusiasm and interest for these subjects. Develop intense powers of attention and concentration to memorise and study effectively.

Belonging. This is sometimes called the 'holistic method'. The mind likes to get an overview of a topic before it starts filling in the details. Just as we tackle a jigsaw puzzle. We look at the illustration and then start working from the outer edges and work our way inwards. We are using a telescopic approach going from less detail to more detail. Psychologists call this the 'gestalt' approach. Of course, Mind Maps are an application of this idea.

Recency/primacy. Recency means we remember better what we did last, that is, most recently. Primacy means we remember better what we did first rather than what came subsequently. We remember our first day at school, our first day at work, our first love affair etc. This is the novelty concept and the reason why as a child you learnt so well. Things are impressed on your memory when they are new and novel. So when studying a subject for the first time consciously make as much use of the novelty concept as possible. The recency/primacy principle suggests the more starts and finishes in a study period the better. Of course, after each study period take a five minute break. To maintain your level of concentration keep your study sessions to one hour's duration or less with short rests inbetween for review and consolidation of information. Immediately after you have learnt something is the time when your memory for it is best. This is called the 'reminiscence effect'. Frequent breaks allow you to take advantage of this.

Effect. This is the 'Pygmalion effect'. Educationalists have found that praise produces greater effort than criticism. Thus a little praise now and again will reinforce your motivation to succeed. By the way, don't wait around for other people to praise you. Self-stroking or praising yourself is a type of auto-suggestion and is nearly as effective. This also builds up your self-esteem and powers of positive thinking. The 'Pygmalion effect' suggests that students live up to a role model expectations of them. So if you have a teacher who treats you as an intelligent, mature and able person and sets you high standards of performance you are likely to live up to their expectations.

Feelings of competition often intensify the study effort. This phenomenon is well known to Training Managers who use the case study method to get participants competitively and imaginatively involved in the learning process. This suggests that it might be more productive to form study groups.

Stand out (outstanding). In psychology this is called the Von Restorff effect. If you want to recall something make it unique and outstanding. Remember the 'MUSE' principle? MUSE is a mnemonic standing for movement, unusualness, slapstick and exaggeration. In other words, if you want to remember something visualise it in an unusual context, using vivid imagination, colour, exaggeration, and humour. This will make the information more memorable.

The 'PLAN' system of memory

PLAN is a mnemonic which stands for the main systems of memory. These are:

Place system

Link system

Alphabet system

Number rhyme and number shape.

The place system

The basic idea in the place system is to use the items of furniture in each room in your home as hooks to associate or link things to. The hooks might be door, lamp, window, clock, chair, table, plant, tv, cabinet and fireplace. Associate the items you want to remember with these links. Then when you want to remember them you take a mental walk around your house picking off the items as you go around.

It is easier to associate items with familiar pegs, which is the advantage of the room system. It is also expandable in relation to the number of rooms and items in each room in your home. The pegs can also be items you encounter on a familiar walk or car journey. For abstract items you may have to use substitute concrete words. An example, of this would be say Justice, Liberty and Fraternity. To remember these just think of a judge, the statue of liberty and a group of your relatives who have turned up unexpectedly. Visualise the judge sitting on your favourite fireside chair, the statue of liberty on top of the tv and your relatives sitting on the sofa. Use the 'MUSE' principle to imprint the items on your memory – movement; unusualness; slapstick and exaggeration.

The link system

This uses your powers of vivid imagination to associate items together in sequence. Again use the MUSE principle when doing so. In other words, see things in an action related context; larger than life; millions of them; in a humorous situation and in colour. As an example, say you want to remember dog, television, pencil and apple. Just picture the dog devouring the tv, the tv with pencils stuck out of the screen and apples being knifed with pencils. The more vivid and unusual the association the better you'll recall it.

Alphabet system

In your early school days you committed to memory the 26 letters of the alphabet. This means that you have 26 hooks for associating things to. The idea here is to invent words to represent each letter of the alphabet and commit these to long-term memory. For example, A might be axe; B might be bee; C might be sea; D might be deed and so on. So if you want to remember 26 items you link or associate them with these ready-made hooks.

Number rhyme

The number rhyme is a well known memory system used in scores of memory books. It goes like this: 1 is gun; 2 is shoe; 3 is tree; 4 is door; 5 is hive; 6 is sticks; 7 is heaven; 8 is gate; 9 is wine; 10 is hen. The same principle of associating items you want to remember with these easily recallable hooks is used.

Number shape

The number shape is based on the idea of animated digits. The number one here could be a pole; two could be a swan; three could be a butterfly; four could be a sailing boat; five could be a sickle; six could be a snake in the form of a six; seven could be the bow of a ship; eight could be an hourglass; nine could be a walking stick; and ten could be a bat and ball. These could be used as hooks or could be substituted for numbers. So to recall 26 you could visualise a swan devouring a snake.

You won't learn to drive a car by reading a book. Similarly, it takes considerable time, patience and practice to get proficient in the PLAN system of memory. Nevertheless your efforts will be more than adequately rewarded by the development of an outstanding memory in your area of expertise. Nothing worthwhile is easy to learn and master. So start now, practise and persevere.

Keep words concrete!

Making memory mnemonics

Mnemonics have been used throughout this book as they are very useful when trying to jog memory. Don't overdo them, however, or you'll have a job trying to remember the mnemonics! Use them sparingly for greater effect. The rhyme 'thirty days hath September ... helps us to remember the number of days there are in each month of the year. A well-known mnemonic for remembering the chemical constituents of coal is NO CASH where N stands for Nitrogen, O for Oxygen, C for Carbon, A for Ash, S for Sulphur and H for Hydrogen.

If you find it difficult to get the letter combinations to make up words, use an aid such as *The Word Game Winning Dictionary* by Bruce Wetterau, or other 'Scrabble' aid word books. Also, a good dictionary and a *Roget's Thesaurus* are indispensable. Use mnemonics and visual imagination to put fun back into learning, making it personalised, exciting and enjoyable, as it should be.

A mnemonist is a person with a trained memory. Why not use some of the devices these experts use? Some examples of mnemonics are:

- PEST which is used for environmental analysis. This stands for **P**olitical, **E**conomic, **S**ocial and **T**echnological.

- PAIN which is used for recalling the various investment appraisal methods. This stands for **P**ayback, **A**ccounting rate of return, **I**nternal rate of return and **N**et present value.

- PLOCS recalls the main functions of management. This stands for **P**lanning, **L**eading, **O**rganising, **C**ontrolling and **S**taffing.

- SREDIM is the work study approach to solving problems. This nonsense word stands for **S**elect, **R**ecord, **E**xamine, **D**evelop, **I**nstall and **M**aintain. This can also be adapted and used to recall the key steps in the problem solving or decision-making process.

- AIDA stands for **A**ttention, **I**nterest, **D**esire and **A**ction and is an aspect of sales promotion.

- DAGMAR stands for **D**efining **A**dvertising **G**oals for **M**easured **A**dvertising **R**esults.

- SPEWSIC is a nonsense word which will help you remember the strategic planning process: **S**trategic objectives; **P**osition audit; **E**nvironmental analysis; **W**OTS UP analysis; **S**trategies to fill the gap; **I**mplementation and **C**ontrol.

- SMART may be used to help you remember the characteristics of good objectives. They should be **S**pecific; **M**easurable; **A**ttainable; **R**ealistic and **T**imely.

- APES may help you remember the major controls in a business. This mnemonic stands for **A**nnual plan control; **P**rofitability control; **E**fficiency control and **S**trategic control.

To remember the names of the planets in our solar system use the sentence 'My Very Educated Mother Just Showed Us Nine Planets'. This stands for Mercury, Venus, Earth, Mars, Jupiter, Saturn, Uranus, Neptune and Pluto. The colours of the rainbow can easily be remember by 'Richard Of York Gave Battle In Vain'. This stands for Red, Orange, Yellow, Green, Blue, Indigo and Violet.

You probably came across the memory device for remembering that stalactites hang on the ceiling of caves (c for ceiling and tights down) while stalagmites come from the cave floor up (g for ground and mites up). Principle and principal are two words which are often misspelt and confused. To remember them for all time learn 'principle is a rule while principal is a pal'. If you have problems remembering how to spell 'believe' just remember 'never believe a lie'. To distinguish 'stationery' from 'stationary' just visualise a large Envelope for stationery. Why not invent your own mnemonics for critical areas of your studies or work, or for vital information that you need to remember? Research shows that when people are given only a short time to study a list, those using mnemonics learn two to three times better than those who use their usual approach.

Systematic use of memory for examinations

'Memory is the receptacle and sheath of all knowledge'. *Cicero*

Initially, in any subject there are basic facts you must acquire before you can progress to a higher level of understanding. The following systematic approach to the learning and memorisation of these facts is recommended;

1. For each subject and from study up of to ten previous past-examination papers and the syllabus, identify key areas and topics which recur.

2. Identify the important definitions (about half a dozen) facts and concepts in these areas.

3. Write definitions on cards. Put these in alphabetical order and take them around with you for revision during spare moments of the day.

4. Invent mnemonics for topical examination issues using key words only and practise as in (3). For related topics link the mnemonics to form sentences or create a little story for maximum recall.

5. Have sets of cards for each subject. Designate certain days of each week on a rotational basis for each subject area. For example: Monday (financial management), Tuesday (company law), Wednesday (management) and so on.

6. Prepare Mind Maps of mnemonics covering an integrated area of each subject. Use these to establish links between topics. This will help you develop your powers of knowledge, comprehension, application, analysis, synthesis, evaluation and problem solving.

7. Practice makes perfect. Practice makes permanent. Overlearning will make vital information part of your own thought process enabling you to apply it to particular examination problems as necessary.

Memory and drugs

When studying always be alert. Alertness and concentration are vital to successful studying. Alcohol and drugs, apart from destroying brain cells, also impede concentration and should not be taken when studying. The odd cup of tea or coffee will help you keep alert. Try to keep physically fit and keep to a nutritious diet as maintaining health is an important aspect of studying.

Video and audio cassettes

Watch the Open University programmes on BBC Television and business programmes generally on television for lectures and topics relevant to your syllabus. The Open University has many excellent lectures on economics, management, accountancy, finance, information technology and so on. If you have a video recorder some of these programmes might be worth recording for review purposes. In any event, you might be able to persuade the training officer in your company to hire or purchase some of the better lectures from the BBC or elsewhere for viewing and discussion by your study group. There is now a wide variety of examination related topics available on cassette tapes. Use these as appropriate for study and revision. If your company has an open learning centre, use it. There are now very good computer-based training packages on all aspects of business.

Summary

The mnemonic 'OPTIMISTIC' will help you recall most of the memory aids in this chapter. It stands for:

Ongoing recall

Pose questions

Techniques (PLAN – place, link, alphabet, number rhyme, number shape systems)

Interest

Mnemonics

Integrate into your life

STM v LTM

Thinking/reflection

Imagination and visualisation

Categorisation and chunking

Be optimistic about your ability to develop a good memory. Believe in yourself. If you think you can, you will. If you think you can't, you won't. Practise the memory techniques outlined in this chapter.

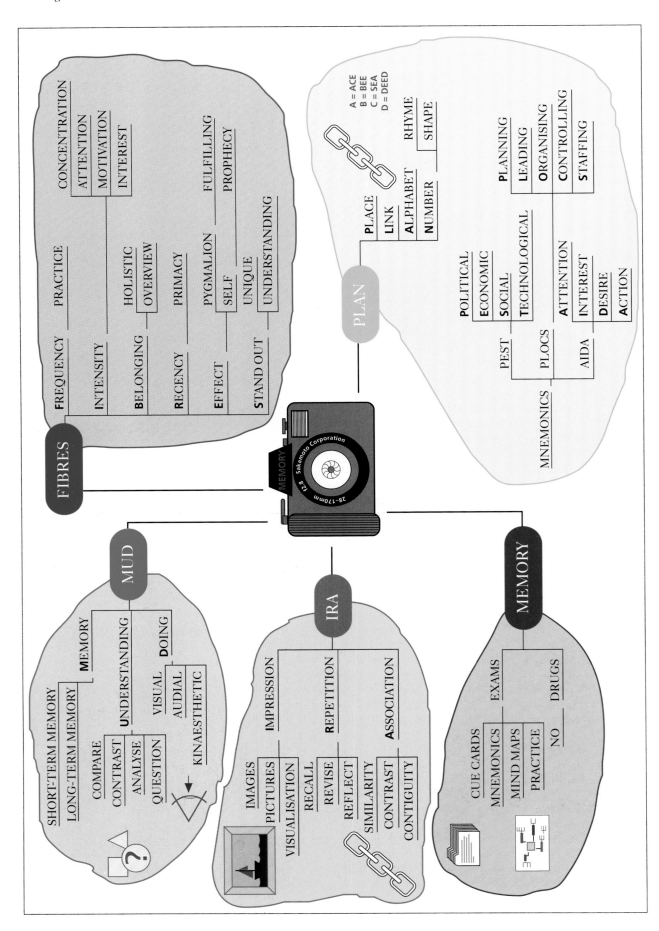

6
Case Studies

What is the rationale behind case studies?
What is the systematic approach to tackling case studies?
How can I apply this to gain more marks when answering case studies?
What are the three main faults examiners find with students in answering case studies?

'It is not enough to have a good mind. The main thing is to use it well.' *René Descartes*

Introduction

Case studies are now being used in university and professional examinations to test students' ability to apply their knowledge in a practical context.

Case studies are designed to test your powers of absorption, comprehension, conceptualisation, application, integration, analysis, synthesis, judgement, creativity, communication and evaluation. The examiner is trying to test your ability to apply your studies to problems in a logical, analytical, practical and systematic fashion. Are you aware of the causes of the problems before selecting the possible solutions?

Information given in case studies is often incomplete, simulating the type of situation that managers are faced with daily in practice, when they have to come to decisions based on incomplete facts and under exacting time constraints. Similarly in the examination room you will be dealing with open-ended cases with insufficient information and incomplete facts while working to a strict time deadline. To do this you must be able to integrate, adapt and apply your knowledge to the particular problem that any question describes.

You need to have:

1. a flexible approach;
2. realistic opinions;
3. practical recommendations.

For example, marketing, business management and strategic planning questions, unlike management accounting questions, do not have a correct numerical answer, and it would usually be wrong and wasteful of valuable time to look for a correct or complete answer in any figure work that you do. In a recent examiners' report, the examiner writes:

'The management accountant has to know how to extrapolate from the data at hand to obtain the information needed. Where critical variables cannot be quantified he may have to point to assumptions included in his analysis or provide guidance as to its sensitivity.'

Case studies are therefore open-ended and assumptions have to be made about missing and incomplete information.

SREDIM

There is a well-known approach to solving problems which can be recalled by the mnemonic SREDIM. This approach is as follows:

Select. Select the problem for study. Make sure that you understand what the real problem is.

Record the facts given. Differentiate between facts, assumptions and opinions.

Examine, analyse and interpret. Adopt a critical, questioning and sceptical attitude as appropriate. Examine the Purpose – What is done? Why is it done? What else might be done? What should be done? Person – Who does it? Why does that person do it? Who else might do it? Who should do it? Place – Where is it done? Why is it done there? Where else might it be done? Where should it be done? Sequence – When is it done? Why is it done then? When might it be done? When should it be done? Means – How is it done? Why is it done that way? How else might it be done? How should it be done?

Develop alternative solutions. Flexibility of mind and creativity is needed here. In how many different ways could this problem be solved?

Implement. Choose and put into operation the best alternative.

Maintain. Maintain and follow up to ensure that your solution has worked out satisfactorily.

Systematic approach to case studies

First read through the case study quickly to familiarise yourself with the case. Then read it in detail applying the systematic approach to case studies as follows.

Identify the problem

Identify the problem, or problems, and issues involved. Identify the real problem. Einstein wrote 'The formulation of a problem is far more essential than its solution, which may be merely a matter of mathematical or experimental skill. To raise new questions, new possibilities, to regard old problems from a new angle, requires creative imagination.' Do not confuse the symptoms with the problem. For example, an influenza virus causes a headache, sore throat, sneezing, tiredness, perspiration and aching joints. These are symptoms – the action of a virus is the problem. However, identifying the symptoms may help you to identify the problem.

What is a problem? In very simple terms it's the difference (the gap) between an actual situation and some desired state. In strategic management this is called gap analysis, the gap being the difference between the existing or extrapolated position and the corporate objective. The gap is filled by the implementation of appropriate strategies.

The first step is to understand the existing situation as given in the case study. In strategic planning this is called the position audit or situation analysis. The second step is to compare this with the desired state in which the organisation would prefer to be. Remember there is likely to be more than one problem facing an organisation. The position audit under the eight Ms' classification may help you to identify the major problem categories. The eight Ms' stand for **M**anpower, **M**oney, **M**aterials, **M**achines, **M**anagement, **M**anagement structure and culture, **M**arketing and **M**anagement information systems. You should state the problems as precisely as possible. All problems will not be of equal importance. So you must prioritise your list of problems focusing in on the solution of those with the greatest payoff.

Problems are usually interlinked and interact and affect each other in a complex multifaceted manner. For example, many case studies are usually written around specific issues. The problem for solution is normally set out by the examiner in the questioning approach – what is the problem (or problems)? Where does it occur? When does it occur? Whose problem is it? Why does the problem occur? What are the reasons for the problem? How can the problem be overcome?

In business organisations problems may be caused at corporate, functional or line level, inter alia, by poor performance or standards in planning, leadership, motivation, control, communication, co-ordination, setting objectives, time management, delegation, interpersonal relationships, interdepartmental conflicts, organisational politics, discipline and many more. Remember that a problem well stated is half-way to being solved.

Identify the real problem.

Study the facts

Record and summarise the facts given. Focus on the facts appropriate to the solution of the questions asked. More important, identify the facts that are not given but that in practice would need to be taken into account for a good decision. Why do case study writers leave out information or give incomplete information? There are three possibilities.

1. The information may have been unobtainable.

2. It was left out deliberately because its omission made for a better and more focused case study. Logistical information may have been excluded because the casewriter wished students to concentrate on the strategic and organisational aspects of the case. Production and personnel information may be excluded because the casewriter wanted to focus the examinee's attention on the marketing issues. Students sometimes think that because certain information is not provided it is irrelevant. This is not a wise assumption.

3. In some examinations, case studies must be kept to a reasonable length because of the time limitation. Information, therefore, is not included because of the necessity to keep the case study short. This would suggest that only essential information is given, peripheral information being excluded. Therefore, missing information may have to be assumed or extrapolated by the student.

If faced with a similar problem in a work situation how would you solve it? This will force you to consider the practical implications and constraints associated with the problem. Where figures are provided they may also be incomplete.

Examiners' reports are invaluable sources of guidance on exactly what is required. For example, recently an examiner in management made the following pertinent comments:

'The case-study type questions in Section A are intended to test candidates' ability to relate theoretical knowledge to the situations described. The four main sources of error were:

(a) Failing to absorb, or ignoring, the information given. Each item of information in the situation should be carefully considered, its relevance to the question determined and its implication deduced.

(b) Making assumptions about missing information. As in real life, the information is usually incomplete. Students must avoid unsubstantiated assumptions but should take into account uncertainties.

(c) Some of the conclusions drawn from the information were so absurd that it can only be assumed that the candidates have studied or revised a limited number of topics and convince themselves. at first glance that the case is about one of them. The information is then distorted to fit this view.

(d) Misinterpretation of the information. The question revealed a number of areas where candidates appear to have difficulty in relating practice to theory.'

Examine the facts

Some analysis, classification, reclassification and interpretation of the facts may be appropriate and necessary to help you arrive at worthwhile decisions. When case studies are complex it is difficult to keep all aspects of the problem in mind at once. The mind span of attention is only between five and nine items. You should, therefore, group data to keep it within the time span of attention. Use mind maps, tables, graphs, algorithms, diagrams and flowcharts as appropriate for this.

Apply problem-solving techniques, where applicable, such as ratio analysis, decision trees, discounted cash flow, marginal costing, breakeven analysis, gap analysis, growth share matrix, directional policy matrix, SWOT analysis, the product life cycle and so on. Application of the Organisation and Methods questioning approach (Purpose; Person; Place; Sequence and Means) discussed previously may give you a greater insight and facilitate closer analysis of the problem. Display to the examiner that you can integrate and apply the concepts, knowledge and theory from your course to the practical requirements of the case study.

Develop alternatives

This is the creative stage of the problem-solving sequence. One source of inspiration should be your own experience. This may be from your own work experience in an organisation, your leisure time experience of being a member of a voluntary or professional organisation or your everyday experience of dealing with other organisations as a customer. How would these organisations solve the problem? Novel solutions, provided they are sensible, acceptable and practical may also win you good marks. Brainstorming and lateral thinking are well-known methods for coming up with original ideas. Use a Mind Map to get your ideas down on paper and to show the interrelationships between different ideas.

In specialised fields such as financial accounting, management accounting, financial management, management, economics, strategic planning and marketing and so on, there are well known tried and tested standard procedures, techniques and models for solving problems. For example, in marketing you might use the product market strategies of market penetration, market development, product development and diversification.

In addition, you might consider positioning, segmentation, niche, marketing mix and pricing strategies for different stages of the product life cycle. In management you might consider delegation, improving the span of control, reducing the number of levels in the scalar chain, encouraging team spirit, improving controls, training and development and so on. In strategic management you might consider organic growth or growth by acquisition (horizontal, vertical, concentric or conglomerate). Other strategies might include joint venture, franchising, divestment, corporate venturing or a management buyout.

Pick the best alternative(s)

Having considered the alternative strategies that the company should pursue then pick the best alternative. Obviously, there are many alternative solutions to any problem. Therefore, you should rank alternatives in terms of their benefits. Look at the pros and cons of each. Eliminate the impractical and less profitable. Risk and uncertainty should also be taken into account. Qualitative outcomes of solutions should be considered.

The criteria for the best alternative should include cost benefit analysis, practicability and acceptability of the proposed solution to the case study under examination. What is the effect on the bottom-line result? To be worthwhile the overall profitability, effectiveness and efficiency of the organisation should improve.

Implement the solution

Describe how you would do this in practice, for example, via delegation, training and development, improved communication channels, counselling and reorganisation. List the types of problems, constraints and obstacles that may be encountered and have to be overcome in practice when an attempt is made to sell and implement the solution, for example, limited resources of staff and time, staff resistance to change, trade union objections, company policy and so on. When will implementation take place? How will it be done/who will do it? How much will it cost?

What would be the corporate, financial, production, personnel, marketing, organisational, behavioural, customer and competitive implications of implementing the strategy? What contingency plans should you make to overcome likely problems?

Monitor and follow up

Monitor and follow up to see that the implemented solution has proved to be as successful as intended and also to learn from problems encountered and shortcomings highlighted. Say how you would do this in practice.

Remember the management of time is just as important when answering case studies as when answering more conventional examination questions.

The three main faults in answering case studies

In a recent examiners' report for a major professional body, the examiner mentioned three main faults exhibited by candidates in answering case studies as follows.

1. Wasting time by restating the information given in the question.
2. Failing to draw conclusions which logically followed from the information.
3. Making totally unjustified assumptions about the situation described. This in turn is likely to lead to quite irrelevant answers.

Summary

Case studies are now used by many third level examinations to test students' ability to apply knowledge to practical situations. The systematic approach to answering case studies is:

- overview;
- identify the problem, or problems, and issues involved;
- record and summarise the facts given;
- examine the facts;

- develop alternative solutions to the problem;
- choose the best alternative/alternatives;
- implement the solution;
- monitor and follow up;
- apply time management principles.

The mnemonic SREDIM will help you remember the systematic approach to the solution of case study problems.

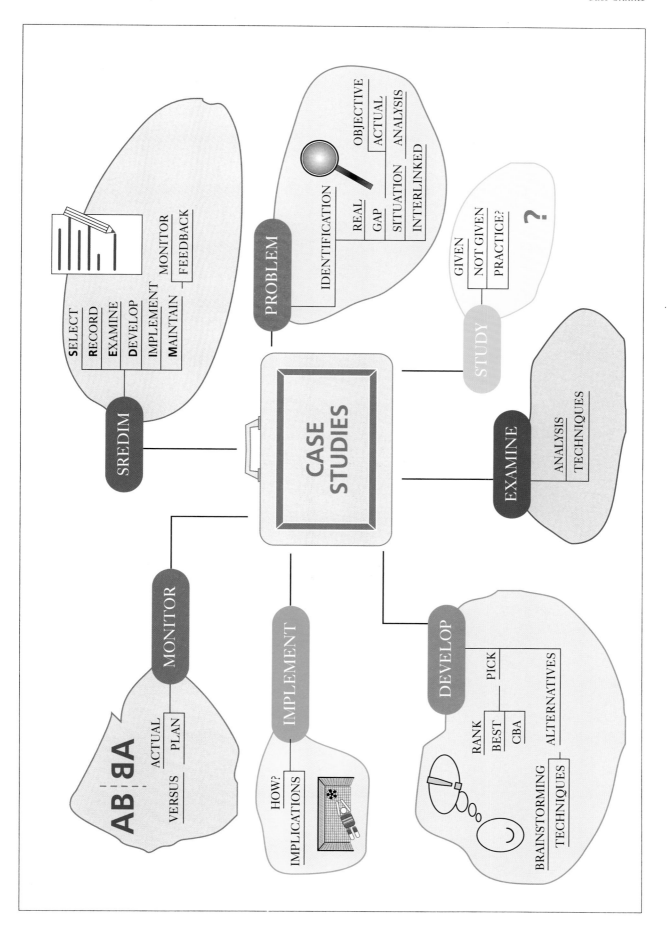

CASE STUDIES

SREDIM
- SELECT
- RECORD
- EXAMINE
- DEVELOP
- IMPLEMENT
- MAINTAIN
  - MONITOR
  - FEEDBACK

PROBLEM
- IDENTIFICATION
  - REAL
  - GAP
  - SITUATION
  - INTERLINKED
  - OBJECTIVE
  - ACTUAL
  - ANALYSIS

STUDY
- GIVEN
- NOT GIVEN
- PRACTICE?

EXAMINE
- ANALYSIS
- TECHNIQUES

DEVELOP
- BRAINSTORMING
- TECHNIQUES
- ALTERNATIVES
  - RANK
  - BEST
  - CBA
  - PICK

IMPLEMENT
- HOW?
- IMPLICATIONS

MONITOR
- ACTUAL
- PLAN
- VERSUS

7

Tips on Presentation

Why is presentation so important?
What are the basic rules of good presentation?
How can I apply these rules to gain more marks in the examination?

'If the story of the Creation can be told in 400 words, if the Ten Commandments contain only 297 words, if Lincoln's immortal Gettysburg Address was only 266 words, if an entirely new concept of freedom was set up in the Declaration of Independence in about 1,300 words – it is up to some of us to use fewer words, and thus save the time, energy, vitality, and nerves of those who must read or listen.' *Jerome P. Fleishman*

Importance of presentation

All the professional examinations and university degree programmes now highlight the importance of presentation. In the rubric to one major accountancy body's examinations the following is stated:

'Answer the question using:

- effective arrangement and presentation;
- clarity of explanation;
- logical argument;
- clear and concise English.'

Similarly the other professional bodies are placing greater emphasis on written presentation skills. The development of all-round presentation skills is important in most professions. The next section deals specifically with the basic rules of good written presentation.

Effective arrangement and presentation

Break up your answer into paragraphs. A paragraph is a group of sentences forming an idea. Answers may have anything from three to ten paragraphs or more. For effect, you should vary the length of your paragraphs. Drop a line between each paragraph for better visual presentation. Also, signpost each paragraph with a title (i.e. the key idea). Paragraphs should be developed and sequenced in a logical order which demonstrates to the examiner that you are working to a plan.

The first sentence of your paragraph is the topic sentence. This indicates clearly what the paragraph is about and helps you stick to the point. Now develop your main point by explanation, analysis, illustration and example.

The subject matter of your paragraph should be organised in a coherent and concise manner. Points within each paragraph should flow and evolve logically and naturally from the ideas presented.

Your final paragraph should be an effective conclusion following logically from the preceding paragraphs. Indecisiveness is not the hallmark of a professional. Mere summarisation is a waste of time and will win you no further marks.

As appropriate use headings, subheadings, indentations, underlining, listing and numbering of points within answers to enhance presentation.

Remember, there is nothing more irritating to the eye than one long unbroken, homogeneous answer. The examiner is put off even before reading the script. Hence the importance of paragraphing.

Clarity of explanation

Develop an individual style

Writing is a creative process. So develop your own style. Avoid the trite or well-worn phrases which should have no place in an examination. Thinking in terms of the reader means adapting your style and the content of your answer to the examiner's requirements. In presenting a case write impersonally and authoritatively. Avoid saying 'I think that' or 'in my opinion'. Better to say that 'some management theorists consider that'. Be objective; your political opinions or views are not required. A layman's answer is not good enough. The examiner wants you to demonstrate the fact that you have read the required books and followed the recommended course of study.

Meaning

An ambiguous word or sentence is one which is open to a number of interpretations. You should therefore choose the appropriate technical word for the job. Be sure that your answer makes sense. Try to visualise yourself as the examiner and imagine how you would react to the script if you were examining it. After all, the examiner is an expert in this area. Therefore, the precise technical language of the discipline should be used as appropriate. This highlights the importance of building up your vocabulary of the technical terms used in the subject area. These are the building blocks that you need to help you write with clarity and precision.

Grammar

In addition, apply the main rules of grammar and use words in their correct sense. Good punctuation will help make your sense completely clear. Two people can only understand each other if they use words and phrases that belong to accepted good English.

To quote from an economics examiner:

> *'Sometimes sentence construction is so bad, or explanation so confused, that it is impossible to determine what the candidate is trying to say. What cannot be interpreted cannot be marked.'*

Logical argument

Problem identification

Accurate identification of the problem, proper analysis and succinct presentation of conclusions are all required for successful professional work. Therefore answers must be structured and logically thought out. Point B should be developed and follow logically from point A. Concepts, arguments, theories, ideas and practical implications should be organised and linked in a logical sequence.

Follow question structure

The answer should follow the structure implicit in the question. Underline the key words in the question before beginning your answer. Key words from the question should be incorporated in your answer to show the examiner that you have read and clearly understood the question. Technical terms should be defined comprehensively to help you develop your answer. Avoid contradictions and unsupported statements which do not follow from the facts presented.

Lengthy, undisciplined, repetitive answers containing wild speculation and invalid assumptions will suggest to the examiner that little time has been spent thinking about the question and its implications. This not only wastes valuable time but gains few marks. Relevancy is the key to success in answering exam questions. Conclusions should be derived logically from the case made. Candidates should never assume that points will be inferred from their answers. They should, instead, always explain fully the development, source and reasons for their thinking.

Clear and concise English

Clear and precise

Clarity of mind is usually evidenced by clarity both in speech and in the written word. On the other hand, a student's lack of understanding is often camouflaged by verbosity and long-windedness. Precision and clarity of expression will prevent misrepresentation and misinterpretation. Words have different shades of meaning. Be sure to use those which communicate precisely the meaning intended. Finally, remember the four Cs of good writing: clarity, correctness, conciseness and coherence.

Be concise

Why use many words when a few will do the job just as well? The examiner who is working to a deadline does not have all day to wade through your padded material. After all he has hundreds more scripts to get through and he only gets paid the same fee for each. The examiner will normally strike out pages of verbiage and waffle. Non-answers in the form of tautological statements such as 'Accrued expenses are expenses which have been accrued' are wasteful of time and will earn no marks. Therefore, be selective in the points you make and the words you use.

Why, therefore, make the job more difficult for the examiner than it has to be? The solution, of course, is to be brief, clear, simple, legible and direct. Brevity has been defined as words that cover more ground than they occupy. Get quickly and directly to the point. The following are some examples of verbose phrases and the suggested shorter equivalents:

Verbose phrases	*Concise phrases*
In the normal course	normally
In view of the fact that	because
In the near future	soon
At the present time	now
In spite of the fact that	although
Make a revision	revise

To quote an examiner:

> *'Candidates often lacked the ability to express themselves concisely and consequently wrote at length in expressing a single point.'*

Keep your sentences short

Clarity does not automatically follow on from brevity, although, generally speaking, being brief does enhance clarity. Bear in mind, however, that you can be too brief as well. A happy medium is desirable. Therefore, vary the length of your sentences. This puts variety in your style and makes your writing thoughtful, interesting and pleasing to the eye. On the other hand, being long-winded is often synonymous with confused and woolly thinking.

Readability

Dr Flesch, author of *The Art of Readable Writing*, recommends that the average sentence should be about seventeen words long. If your sentences are more than twenty words long, you should beware. Experts also recommend that you should keep your word count to at least 70 per cent one-syllable words for greater readability. Readability then is determined by the choice of words used, the length of sentences and the clarity and conciseness of expression. This is not always practical when technical terminology is appropriate but is nevertheless a good guiding principle to abide by.

Spelling is as important as expression.

Good spelling

Professional examinations are not a test of spelling. However, good professionals as well as being able to express themselves, should also be able to spell. For example, to quote an economics examiner:

> '*Spelling mistakes abounded: aspiring managers should not be writing entrapreneur, competative, oppertunity, shoping, comodity, summerised and suppermarket – all examples from the current scripts.*'

The following are some more words that are commonly misspelt.

Correct spelling	Often misspelt as
Accommodation	Accomodation
Beginning	Begining
Competence	Competance
Definition	Defination
Feasible	Feasable
Interrupted	Interupted
Relevant	Relevent
Separate	Seperate
Successfully	Sucessfully

You should also try to avoid confusing principle with principal, access with assess and so on. Make your own list of problem words which you frequently misspell or confuse with other words. Study and eliminate these mistakes from your life once and for all time. Acquire and use a good dictionary to help you in your efforts.

Summary

Presentation skills are very important for potential accountants and other professionals. Good presentation skills can make the difference between a pass and a marginal failure in examinations. It therefore pays to develop your presentation skills. The basis of good presentation skills is:

- effective arrangement and presentation;

- clarity of explanation;

- logical argument;

- clear and concise English;

- good spelling;

- legible handwriting.

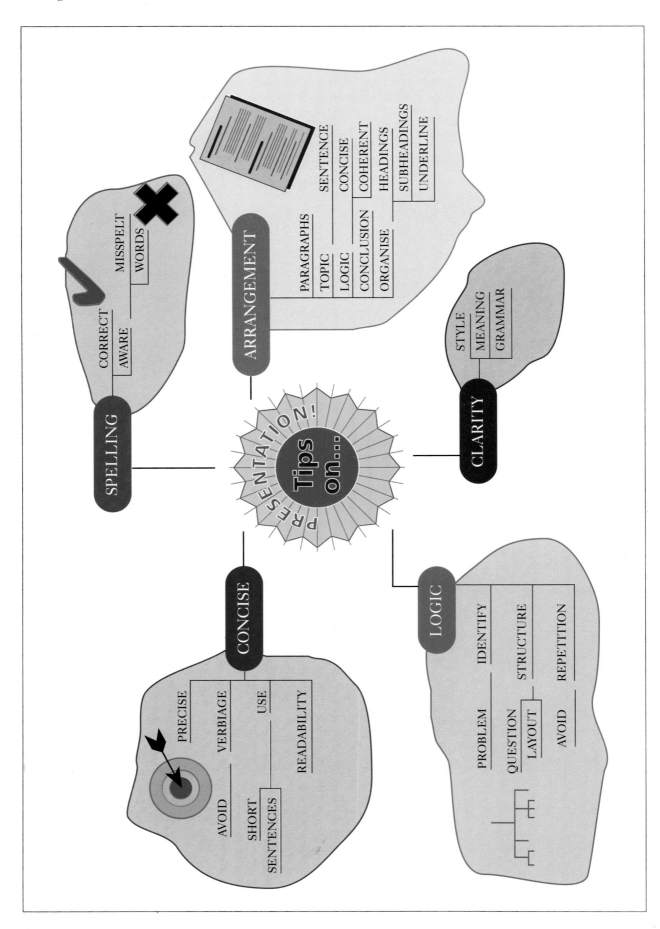

8

Examination Stress

What is examination stress?

How does it affect my concentration and performance in examinations?

What coping strategies can I employ to counteract and control examination stress?

'The mind is its own place, and in itself can make a Heaven of Hell, a Hell of Heaven.' *Milton*

What is examination stress?

Stress can be thought of as an individual's response to threats and challenges in the environment. It can be manifested psychologically or physiologically or both. It is the way you react to and handle stress which determines whether it is good or bad.

Threat to self-esteem

Examination stress results from the potential threat to self-esteem such as loss of face which might arise if you fail. This is caused by individual perception of the gap, whether real or imagined, between the difficulty of the examination and one's capabilities or the difference between your existing state of knowledge and the desired ideal. Some additional anxiety can be brought about through lack of examination preparation. For example, one may not have covered the syllabus adequately and be afraid that something not covered will come up.

Stress results from the possibility of failure.

Less able people become more anxious as exam time draws near than those who are more able. The latter group tend to see examinations as less threatening. It is quite likely that the more significant the examination is to the career prospects of the candidate the more seriously it will be perceived, resulting potentially in higher levels of anxiety being experienced amongst candidates. Parents, fellow students, lecturers and employers can also transmit their anxiety to students thus exacerbating an already tense situation.

Students who have failed an examination on a previous occasion are likely to be more apprehensive and anxious before a resit because they do not wish to go through another humiliating experience. The danger here is that students may be subconsciously conditioning themselves to feeling anxious for all examinations. Do not allow such behaviour patterns to develop into permanent ones, thus becoming part of one's personal baggage.

The good news, however, is that most students forget their anxiety as the examination gets under way. The physical action of writing and the mental activity of concentrating on the here and now reduce stress.

Effects of stress

Psychological

Psychological responses include apprehension, self-doubt, forgetfulness and poor concentration. Unreleased built-up tension can contribute to health problems such as high blood pressure, coronary heart disease, hypertension and cancer. So it pays to combat anxiety not only for examinations but in your lifestyle generally as well.

Excessive worry can have adverse effects on academic performance. The process of preparing for and taking examinations is for most people a stressful affair. Stress often increases as examination time approaches. A certain amount of anxiety is normal. It keeps the adrenalin flowing and may in fact sharpen your concentration powers thereby improving your examination performance.

A high level of anxiety may affect concentration to such an extent that examinees fail to note important examination instructions such as the number of questions and the choices available. This is a common complaint from examiners. In open book examinations examinees have even been known to unintentionally mix up their scripts with their books and take them home.

There is obviously an optimum level of anxiety. A high level is stressful, and hinders concentration, intellectual control and examination performance. A low level is unstimulating and causes lethargy. This has been recognised in the psychological law called the Yerkes-Dodson Law. This states that anxiety improves performance until a certain optimum level of arousal has been achieved. After this point performance deteriorates.

Physiological

Bodily responses to stress include increased heart rate, shortness of breath, trembling hands, shaking legs, palpitations, nausea, sweating, pallor and in some cases fainting. Physical signs such as increased heart rate, increased blood pressure, fatty deposits in the blood and perspiration can be measured scientifically.

High levels of anxiety can also cause physical symptoms such as sleeplessness, headaches, aches and pains, lack of appetite, listlessness, stomach pains and even vomiting.

Coping strategies – examination technique

- *Examination practice*

  Plenty of mock examination practice over a period of time will help to build up your tolerance levels for stress. This will acclimatise you to potential stressful examination situations and will thus help you to counteract them. Anticipation of the forthcoming examination increases the level of anxiety which will be at its worst just before the examination starts. Therefore, it is important to keep your imagination under control, for example by creative visualisation as examination time approaches. The mind cannot accommodate two thoughts at the same time, so whenever a negative thought enters your head, substitute a positive one for it. You can be as positive as you make up your mind to be.

- *Establish a routine*

Follow an established rehearsed routine at the beginning of the examination. Practise the routine of reading the instructions, reading the questions, choosing the ones you are going to attempt and drafting outline answers. Practising this routine in your imagination is just as effective as if done in reality. Develop this skill so that it becomes an automatic response. Then, when the real thing happens it won't bother you. On the principle that forewarned is forearmed, anything which reduces uncertainty and indecision will help control worry.

- *Overlearning*

Some examinees say that their minds go blank inside the examination room. This is probably because they haven't learned the material thoroughly enough. Mastery of the subject matter to the point of overlearning reduces anxiety because the examination is now perceived as being less difficult. Students who are ill-prepared are bound to worry. On the other hand, students who are well prepared actually enjoy and thrive on the experience, which only helps them peak at their maximum performance in the examination room.

- *Creative visualisation*

Mentally train for your examinations. You can practise taking examinations successfully in your own imagination. Rehearse in detail in your own mind the steps involved as a dry run. Psychologists have found this is practically as good as doing the real thing. Athletes use creative visualisation in addition to their normal training to enhance their overall performance. For example, this is an important aspect of a professional boxer's training. In sport it is now accepted that psychological training is just as important as physical training.

- *Study and examination technique*

Developing good habits in this area such as time management, effective reading, memory, mind mapping and presentation skills will help to optimise your performance and reduce worry.

- *Set yourself realistic goals*

Setting yourself the goal of becoming a professional basketball player if you are only five feet tall would certainly be unrealistic. Similarly, if you are very tall it is unlikely that you would make a successful jockey. Have regard to your strengths and weaknesses in setting goals. There is no point in trying to qualify as an accountant, or indeed in any other profession, if you do not possess the appropriate aptitudes and necessary dedication.

Unless you have considerable time, energy, willpower, commitment, application, aptitude and intelligence, trying to complete each stage of a professional accountancy exam in six months may prove a very daunting and stress provoking objective. However, some exceptional people have achieved it. So, unless you are one of these gifted persons it would be better to leave twelve months for each stage and pace yourself accordingly.

Success first time around will reinforce your confidence and motivate you for subsequent parts. Have long, medium, short and immediate term goals. An immediate term goal might be to meet a revision session objective. Little successes create the proper positive mental set and thus build up your confidence.

Coping strategies – mental approaches

- *Motivation*

  If you are an intrinsically motivated student you will probably be able to handle worry better than if you are extrinsically motivated. The former type of student wants to pass the exam because of their wish to satisfy their own needs rather than the wishes or needs of others. The latter worries about what people will think if they fail the examination. This creates further anxiety.

- *Models*

  Find out how successful examinees cope with stress in the examination room. Use these as models to modify your behaviour and control your anxiety levels. People learn by modelling themselves on the successful coping strategies of others.

- *Desensitisation*

  Before the examination think of the things which are likely to cause you anxiety. Now imagine yourself dealing with each of these issues successfully and conclusively in a cool, relaxed and competent fashion. Rehearse this creative visualisation in conjunction with a relaxation technique over a period of time. When the actual examination situation comes round you will behave in a less anxious way. You have learned a relaxed, comfortable association with a situation which previously caused anxiety and even panic.

- *Positive thinking*

  Self-preoccupation and negative thoughts should be avoided. Think of ways in which problems can be solved and difficulties surmounted. Think positively and constructively. Practise positive self-talk rather than negative. Negative self-talk lowers performance and increases worry. Positive self-talk has the opposite effect. Thus positive thinking will eliminate worry and enhance examination performance. Say to yourself that 'I'm going to pass this examination' rather than 'I'm hopeless at exams'. Rehearse in your mind through creative visualisation positive experiences of past examination successes and other achievements. Keep these positive thoughts in your mind. Think success.

- *Laughter is the best medicine*

  Develop a sense of humour. Laughter often provides new perspectives on stressful problems. Laughter is therapeutic. It can relax nerves, improve digestion and help circulation. Learn to laugh at yourself and at life. Try to see the humorous side to life. Watch your favourite comedy on TV and relax.

- *Persistence*

  How many times have you seen students just get up in the middle of the examination and leave? You have no chance at all if you give up so easily. Develop powers of willpower and determination. You should enjoy utilising your willpower and going all out to be successful at your exams. Say to yourself 'My willpower keeps getting stronger. I enjoy using my willpower. It feels good to go all out.' Stick to the task. Give it your best shot.

  If during the examination you have not done as well at a paper as you thought you would, do not give up. It is possible that other candidates found the going just as tough. Be positive about your performance and concentrate on achieving excellence in the next paper.

  Learn from your mistakes. If despite everything you fail, learn from your mistakes by analysing precisely where you went wrong. Develop corrective strategies for the future. Occasional setbacks should strengthen your resolve to be successful next time round. Persistence is the quality that may see you through in the end.

- *Confidence*

This is a belief in one's own ability. For examinations it is the expectation of a successful outcome. Build on your success. Nothing succeeds like success. Failure situations should be avoided. Success reinforces the expectation of success and thus lays the foundation for further achievement. Thus if you are inadequately prepared for an examination do not sit it.

- *Concentration*

This is focused attention or strong thinking activity directed at a limited area so that other areas are simultaneously shut out. Build a wall of concentration around you. Concentrate on the here and now, forget about the past and future. You want to shut out everything except the topic under study. You must become so absorbed in what you are currently doing that you become completely unaware of all other potential distractions. Think about the task rather than about yourself.

Improve concentration through positive self-talk. Developing concentration powers in the examination room must also be learned and practised. Self-talk such as 'I'm beginning to concentrate', 'I'm now concentrating fully' and 'my mind is crystal clear' will condition the mind in the appropriate way. Remember that in the examination room disciplined concentration powers of up to three continuous hours duration are required.

Coping strategies – lifestyle

- *Relaxation*

Use techniques such as meditation, breathing exercises and progressive relaxation methods. Progressive relaxation works by sequentially tensing and relaxing muscles from head to toe. Adopt a comfortable sitting or lying position for these tension reducing exercises. Various forms of breath control can be practised anywhere and help to reduce stress. For example, a well-known breathing exercise is taking a deep breath, holding it and then breathing out – all done in the ratio of 1:4:2. This simple exercise reduces anxiety by optimising oxygen and carbon dioxide levels in the blood. If you want to pursue these ideas further there are many books and cassette tapes available on relaxation techniques in your local bookshop. Listening to your favourite music can also be a great way to unwind and induce a state of relaxation. Likewise, reading a favourite novel can be relaxing.

- *Health*

Sleep, exercise and eating wisely are all ways of keeping a sound mind in a sound body. Vigorous exercise will help you sleep soundly and a balanced, varied diet with adequate fibre will combat stress and fatigue. Eat plenty of fresh fruit as part of your normal diet. Some medical experts recommend that you should drink eight glasses of water a day (dehydration thickens the blood while hydration thins it) and reduce your salt intake as part of any stress management programme. Make sure that you get at least eight hours regular sleep. If you can get by on less you are exceptional.

- *Leisure time*

Many students worry when preparing for professional exams while a tiny minority suffer severe mental stress. A good recuperative antidote to the stress of preparing for and sitting examinations is to have leisure-time activities built into your plan. 'All work and no play makes Jack a dull boy'. More than two thousand years ago Plato said 'Anyone engaged in mathematics or any other strenuous intellectual pursuit should also exercise his body and take part in physical training'. Obviously the ideal leisure-time pursuits should be outdoors with plenty of fresh air and reasonably energetic in order to counteract the sedentary study time activity. Cultural pursuits, such as theatre- and cinema-going, should also be part of your leisure-time activities. These will take your mind off exams and help you relax.

- *Support system*

  It is a good idea to discuss your worries with a trusted friend or family member. A sympathetic ear and a good listener are great antidotes to worry. Just having someone to confide in occasionally can be a great source of peace and comfort.

  Some organisations provide a mentor support system for employees who are studying. If this is available to you, you should use the service. The role of the mentor is to advise, coach, coax, encourage, support, empathise with and generally assist learners. Mentors might be colleagues, supervisors or managers/employees who have themselves completed the degree or qualification being sought. Mentoring provides human contact and a source of support and advice when needed.

  Mentoring also provides an opportunity to build lasting relationships with others in the organisation, and this could aid your career development. There are certain advantages to having a supervisor or manager as mentor: *inter alia*, it will help you to stick to your studies. Being able to negotiate study leave with a sympathetic supervisor is an extra bonus. Employees who have recently completed the examinations may also be willing to act as mentors. They have the added advantage of knowing the problems, pitfalls and anxieties of sitting the exams.

- *Alternative stress*

  Some psychologists feel that your leisure time should be sufficiently different and challenging to provide alternative stress. This should occupy your mind totally so as to counteract by distraction any possibility of preoccupation with study or examination related problems. Leisure-time activities should be built into your programme as a way of rewarding and reinforcing good study practices. There is a positive correlation between physical fitness and peak examination performance.

- *Lifestyle*

  The medical profession has identified a particular type of person who they feel is prone to stress and the related health risks. They have called this type of person the 'A' type. The person who follows a more moderate and less stressful existence they have named the 'B' type. Type 'A' person is always in a hurry (hence the term, hurry sickness), forever trying to meet deadlines. Type 'A' person is very competitive, always has to win and tends to be reactive. Type 'B' person, on the other hand, is more methodical and proactive, is just as ambitious but goes about his work in a less aggressive but nevertheless, systematic, purposeful manner. The Type 'B' student works to a plan, has developed good study skills and is aware of and practises good examination technique. Research has indicated that many chief executives are in fact type 'B' persons. A good model for any ambitious student to imitate!

  The type 'B' person has established correct priorities, practises good principles of time management and as a result achieves the same goals with less hassle and energy output than the frenetic nervous energy output of the type 'A' person. The type 'A' person is more prone to a host of illnesses including stomach ulcers, cancer and heart disease than the type 'B' person.

  From an examination point of view some of the coping strategies outlined will not only help you to be more successful in your examinations but will also establish a more healthy stress free lifestyle for your future. If you want to live a long, happy and healthy life then model your behaviour on the type 'B' person.

Summary

Unmanaged stress lowers attention, concentration and intellectual control. Managed stress, on the other hand, can maximise your performance in the examination room. Coping strategies, which can be used to counteract and control examination stress, have been discussed including:

- examination practice;
- overlearning;
- desensitisation;
- positive thinking;
- relaxation;
- creative visualisation;
- lifestyle;
- support system;
- having realistic goals.

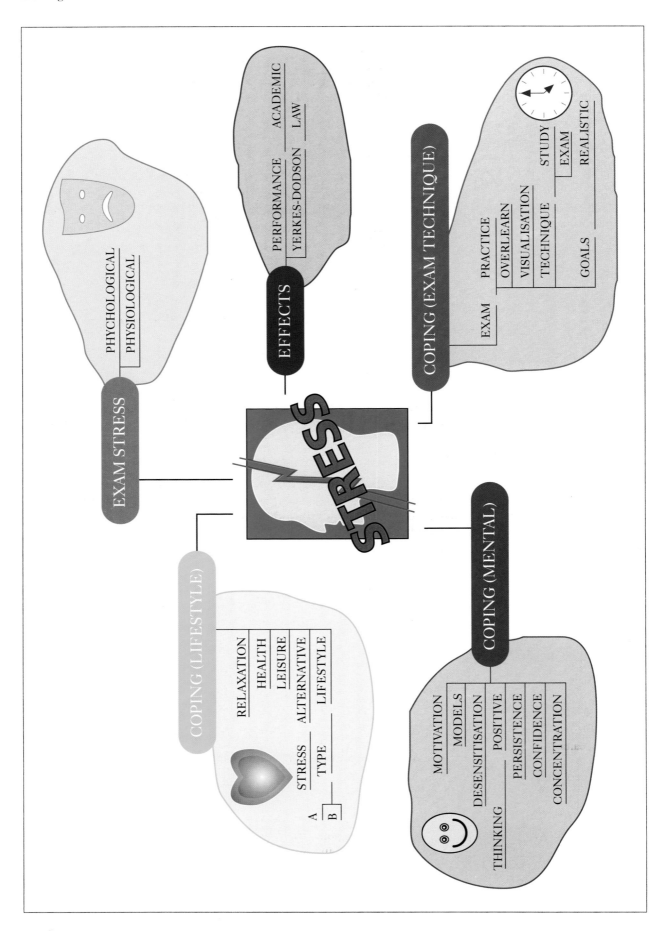

9

Examination Faults

What are the common examination faults?
What are some of the specific exam faults in the computational and narrative areas?
What steps can I take to improve my exam performance in these areas?

'Common sense is not so common.' *Voltaire*

Common faults

Examiners often complain about the following faults, which are caused by, *inter alia*, lack of proper planning.

Layout

1. Deleting phrases, sentences or paragraphs from a script. This looks messy and certainly creates a very unfavourable impression. Only do it if absolutely necessary. In this context do not waste time on rubbing out or using white correcting fluid. Instead, just delete and insert the correction overhead.

2. Inserting material and the frequent use of detailed footnotes.

3. Putting a line through a whole section or page of an answer and starting again.

4. Leaving blank spaces in the middle of an answer hoping for subsequent inspiration. Most examinations prescribe that you start each new question on a fresh page. So if you want to leave a blank space for subsequent inspiration why not leave it at the end of your answer?

5. Answering parts of the same question in several places of the answer book without guidance to the examiner. Remember, practices which make marking more difficult for the examiner are not to be recommended.

6. Failing to use paragraphs, subheadings and indentations as good presentation technique.

Irrelevancy

1. Global, generalised answers when specific information is required.

2. Failure to understand and answer the question set. This could be due to wishful thinking, incorrect reading or misinterpretation.

3. Examinees should not write pleading notes to the examiner to be lenient on them because their careers will be in jeopardy if they do not get a pass. This says little for the maturity of the candidates concerned and only annoys the examiner. This may seem far-fetched but some candidates do resort to such desperate measures.

Time management

1. Answering more than the number of questions required in the belief that the examiner will mark only the best of the answers. This is not so and anyone who has time to answer more will hardly do justice to the others.

2. Not leaving sufficient time to answer all of the questions required. There is a tendency to spend too much time on the first question attempted and too little time on the last.

3. Failure to distribute time in proportion to the marks given. Also, candidates often do not distribute their time within questions in proportion to the marks awarded.

Planning

4. Failure to plan answers before committing thoughts to paper. Quality not quantity is important. Verbosity is no substitute for clear, concise, logical thinking and good presentation.

Specific faults

For our purposes this section will be divided into two broad categories – *computational* or number based subjects and those that are *narrative* or descriptive based. *Computational* includes accounting, quantitative methods, cost accounting, management accounting techniques, financial accounting, business taxation, management accounting and financial management. *Narrative* includes economics, business law, information technology management, management, company law, control and audit and strategic planning and marketing. This classification is for convenience only. Some subjects are both computational and narrative based. Therefore, some examination questions may require a combination of the two.

Usually the computational subjects require more study hours than the narrative type subjects because of the need to develop the practical skills and technical competence required to gain exam standard proficiency. Mere reading of textbooks is not sufficient. For example, in an examiners' report the cost accounting examiner states: 'candidates who marginally failed this paper probably did so because they were not technically competent over the whole syllabus. It is obvious that some candidates (and possibly their tutors) deliberately omit part(s) of the syllabus from their study programmes; this is a dangerous practice which is not to be encouraged.'

Specific faults – computational subjects

Check your answer for reasonableness. Candidates sometimes fail to check their answers to see if they are reasonable and based upon common sense. Examiners are sympathetic to those who evidently understand the principles but who make small slips in arithmetic. They are, however, obviously much less sympathetic when ludicrous or impossible answers are given which could have been rectified if common-sense principles were applied.

Balancing. In subjects like financial accounting do not spend too much time trying to balance. Stick to a planned time allocation. You may still get excellent marks even though your balance sheet or cash flow statement doesn't balance. The approach, layout and application of concepts is much more important than arithmetical accuracy.

Show your workings. Some candidates fail to show intermediate workings when they use a calculator but produce the wrong answer. A proportion of the marks for all questions is reserved for methodology. After all, the rubric will usually state categorically that candidates must clearly show how they have derived their answers from the basic data. They will lose marks if they do not do so even if their answers are correct. The examiner cannot read your mind. Marks will only be awarded for what is shown.

The *explanation/interpretation aspects* of computational questions are sometimes answered very badly. Some candidates are unable to explain principles which they can apply numerically. This would suggest that would-be professionals and business graduates should spend more time developing their written communication skills. For example, in ratio analysis as well as being able to calculate the relevant ratios you must also be able to interpret in words their significance in relation to the question given.

Presentation. Presentation is a very important aspect of quantitative subjects. Good, clear, concise, logical and methodical presentation is expected and marks are reserved for such. The examiner will award marks for apparent logical thinking and understanding even if the result of the calculations is incorrect. For example, budgets are not simply a mass of calculations but should be presented in a tabulated and logical manner. Sloppy layout such as scattering figures in an unco-ordinated way over several pages is not going to endear you to the examiner. Study model answers and published financial statements for good layout practices. A tabular statement or matrix can save you time and earn you extra marks. Appropriate illustrations such as diagrams or graphs can also be very effective. But do remember to label them clearly!

Arithmetic. Poor arithmetic, non-alignment of columns of numbers, careless positioning of decimal points, inaccuracy in simple multiplication are inexcusable for potential accountants and business graduates. Sometimes the inaccurate figures are used to support wrong and often ludicrous conclusions. In this context correctness in basic computational techniques such as compound interest, graphs, bar charts, diagrams and percentages are an essential foundation. Examiners also often complain that candidates are unfamiliar with the use of, say, mathematical tables for students. If your examining body advises use of a particular set of mathematical tables or other aid, ensure that you use it.

Study published accounts. This will give you a feel for the practical real-life world and make you realistic and less dogmatic when answering questions on the interpretation of accounts. It will familiarise you with the best presentation methods as well as the formats required by the Companies Acts and the financial reporting standards. You will also know what value added statements are and will not confuse them with profit and loss accounts or Value Added Tax. Many published accounts also use bar charts, pie charts, graphs and other presentation techniques to illustrate their accounts. Study these to see the various methods and best practices now used to present and illustrate accounting data.

Integrated holistic approach. When answering questions, remember that all areas of your course including previous stages may be relevant. Don't put subjects into pigeon holes. Try to perceive the integrated nature of the course. Particularly at the latter stages of the professional examinations and business degree programmes your ability to integrate knowledge from all areas of the course is examined.

Accounting standards. Know your accounting standards. It is foolhardy going into an examination of a professional accountancy body without knowing these thoroughly, particularly at the later stages of financial accounting.

Taxation. Good, clear, concise, neat and logical presentation with good figure work is essential for this subject. Taxation is a practical and very technical subject. So, as well as having a thorough grasp of your subject you must be able to apply the knowledge to the problems set.

Tax is a technical subject requiring a good detailed knowledge of both taxation principles and law. To quote from a tax examiners' report:

> *'Too many enter the exam hall knowing little about tax but with a determination to fill their workbook by making up the law as they go along.'*

Specific faults – narrative subjects

Law. Law is a technical subject requiring a sound, detailed and precise knowledge of statute and case law. You must display to the satisfaction of the examiner, by the content of your examination script, that you have acquired, understood and can apply this body of knowledge. Common sense, generalisations and a layman's knowledge are not sufficient to pass examinations in law or indeed any other subject.

Specific knowledge. A person seeking professional advice would not appreciate a general reply which did not address the particular problem posed. Answers should be structured with this in mind. To quote from an examiners' report:

'Very short answers necessarily attract few marks. The examiner wants discussion, reference to cases and statutes, and evidence that the candidate has thought about the question and is giving a reasoned answer rather than regurgitation of rote learning.'

Report writing. Reports should be logically sequenced, structured and formatted correctly. They should have a title and a date, and should be addressed to somebody and from somebody. They should be signed at the bottom by the accountant or manager (do not conclude with phrases such as 'Kind regards' or 'Yours sincerely'). Reports should have paragraphs, headings, subheadings, and indentations as appropriate and should finish with a conclusion. Calculations, graphs and tabulations should be relegated to appendices. Terms of reference and summary recommendations should be given at the start of the report. Conclusions should be logically developed and clearly stated. Examiners complain that students often write an essay when asked specifically for report format. It would be well worth referring to any book on report writing in business for guidance in this area.

Information technology management. This paper will test a candidate's real understanding rather than any ability to reproduce rote-learned descriptions of some aspects of information technology. It is difficult to acquire this real understanding without practical hands-on experience. Candidates should, therefore, seize every opportunity to acquire practical experience of using computers and keep up to date generally on information technology. With the spread of personal computers in most organisations, getting direct experience of computers should not be too difficult.

Acquire experience using computers whenever you can.

Spreadsheets. Some companies run in-company courses on computer appreciation, Excel, Lotus 1-2-3, SMART, and other software packages as well as keyboarding skills. Try to get a place on one of these. Take every opportunity to read computer magazines and visit computer hardware and software exhibitions. Also, should you get the chance, visit other companies' computer installations. Develop the skill of flowcharting if you want to do well in these examinations. You should also realise the importance of spreadsheets to accountants and managers in such areas as budgetary control, financial planning, cash flow forecasts, tax planning and so on.

Economics. Economics is a real life practical subject the ramifications of which affect our everyday life. Economic topics are continuously being debated on the television and radio, and also in the daily press and financial journals. However, the popular press approach is not sufficient for these examinations. Instead, read good quality newspapers and journals such as the *Financial Times* and *The Economist*. Show the examiner that you understand the practical implications and significance of what you are studying. Proving that your knowledge extends beyond the recommended texts will help you to impress the examiner.

Economics is the type of subject which lends itself to being illustrated by flowcharts, graphs and diagrams. Frequently, a diagram correctly drawn and properly explained is by far the best way to answer a question in economics. Some questions in fact cannot be answered without clear and accurate diagrams. An example is the relationship of costs and profits. Remember that it is technical knowledge which distinguishes the professional from the layman and that it is the ability to communicate that technical knowledge that will convince the examiner of your professionalism.

Management. The case study type questions are intended to test candidates' ability to relate theoretical knowledge to the situations described. Draw conclusions logically from the information given. Do not make totally unjustified assumptions about the situation described. This will lead to irrelevant answers. The systematic approach to solving case studies recommended in Chapter 6 should be applied. Management like other professions has its own terminology which you must get to grips with.

Summary

There are a number of basic little tips you can apply to specific subjects that will help you maximise your marks in the examinations. However, there is no substitute for adequate expertise gained from study and application of the subject matter. Most of the advice offered is commonsense but commonsense is a rare commodity if one is to judge from the regularity with which these points are addressed in the examiners' reports of the various professional bodies.

Common faults:

- poor layout;

- irrelevant answers;

- poor time management;

- lack of planning.

Specific faults:

- computational errors;

- unreasonable answers;

- no workings;

- lack of an integrated approach;

- lack of technical knowledge.

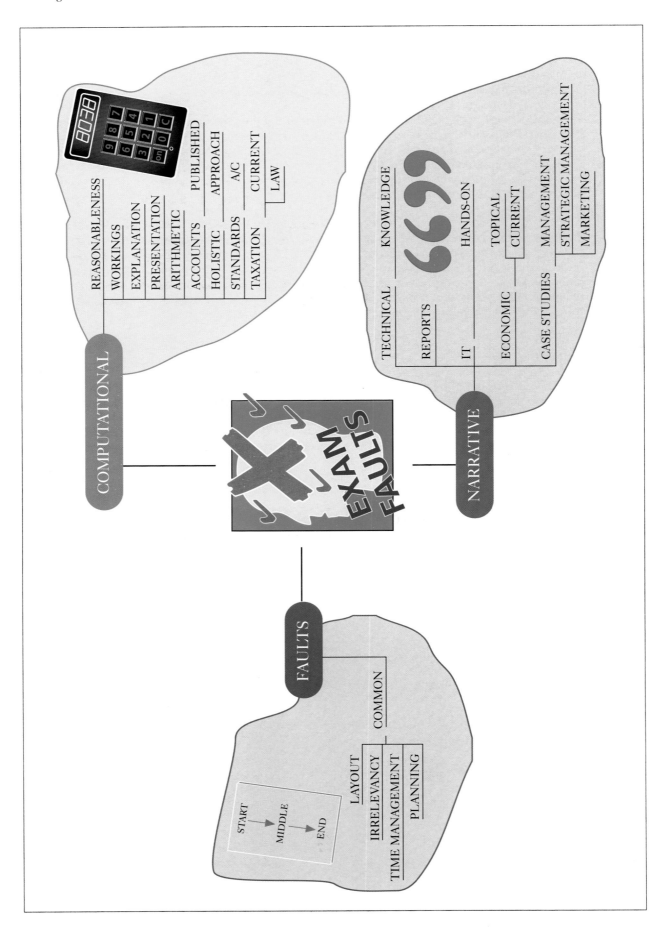

10

Examination Technique

What should I be doing as examination day approaches?
What is the best approach in the examination room?
Why do people fail examinations?
What is the best approach in answering multiple-choice questions?
What are the four basic ingredients for examination success?
What is the RTQPARM approach to answering questions?

'Just as eating against one's will is injurious to health, so study without a liking for it spoils the memory, and it retains nothing it takes in.' *Leonardo da Vinci*

Preparation

You are now aware of and have been systematically applying study techniques, presentation skills and stress management techniques. Plan your review:

1. Have a proper timetable.

2. Space your revision.

3. Variety. Don't study the same topic all night. Alternate subjects to maintain interest and freshness of mind.

4. Recall and revise as indicated in Chapter 5.

5. Employ stress management strategies.

6. Tackle past examination questions, preferably under mock examination conditions. Remember practice makes perfect.

Examination questions

Study old examination papers. See the number of papers there are in the examination. Study the layout of the paper. How many questions are there and how much time is allowed? How many marks are allowed for each paper and for each question? Is there a choice of questions? Are there case studies? Do some questions require a report format answer? Will multiple choice questions be set? All this should be known before you go into the examination room.

Be on the look out for likely examination questions. Draw up a matrix of past topics in your subject to establish trends, if any. There are fashions in academic subjects just as in anything else. Study the relevant professional journals. For example, questions in the examination are frequently on topics featured in professional journals and professional student magazines. Student magazines also feature good articles from time to time on study and examination technique which are always worth a perusal. Pay particular attention to the business section of a quality newspaper or better still read *The Economist* or the *Financial Times*. These will often indicate current topics of interest in the financial world and may very well be the basis of examination questions.

Remember examiners like to cover the whole syllabus in three to four sittings. Therefore, important examination topics which have not come up for the past one or two sittings are probably very likely to come up this time. However, don't take any chances. Cover the syllabus adequately as some questions require the application and integration of knowledge from all of the subject area as well as from more than one area of the overall syllabus. Just pay particular attention to these likely examination topics as the examination date approaches.

Revision

Attempt a mock examination. Sit a past examination paper if possible and get feedback on your performance from your tutor. Devote two weeks before examination time to your private revision work.

Consult your examination syllabus for the areas covered. For example, more than 50 per cent of many professional courses is based on the higher cognitive skills such as conceptualisation, analytical work, identifying and using appropriate techniques, interpretation of results and problem solving. There is now less emphasis than before on number crunching and memory and more on conceptualisation, problem solving and understanding; less emphasis on compilation of figures and more on interpretation of results.

Many professional institutes have published explanatory notes on the abilities required for their syllabus against each examination topic. These should help students decide how much study and revision time should be devoted to each topic.

Syllabus guidance notes. These have been prepared by examiners to assist lecturers and students in preparing for the examinations. They are revised frequently and the latest version should be consulted. Some professional institutes publish these in their professional and student magazines.

Syllabus subject Mind Maps. It is important that the student studies the syllabus very carefully. A Mind Map of each subject area should be drawn up so that the student can see at a glance the range of topics to be covered. It can also be used as a planning and revision tool, items being marked off as they are being studied. By this method there is no chance that complex or unattractive topics will be overlooked by the student.

Make sure that you have covered everything. Avoid re-reading textbooks, manuals or correspondence course notes at this stage. Stick to the Mind Maps, summary Mind Maps and cue cards, and revise definitions, rules, case law and formulae.

The day before. You should use the day before the examination for preparation and a last revision of your Mind Maps or notes. Do not attempt to learn new things at this stage. This last round-up revision will strengthen your memory for the forthcoming event. Do not overdo the revision. Two hours browsing through your Mind Maps should suffice. Go to bed at your normal time. Put your examination equipment in your pocket so that you will be organised in the morning, and don't forget your watch!

Examination centre location

Find out where the examination hall is. Dry run the route in advance so that you know exactly how long it will take you to get there. Build in a contingency allowance for possible traffic holdups. Determine the exact location of the room where the examination is going to be held.

Last minute revision. Arrive at the examination centre in plenty of time. Use your summary Mind Maps and cue cards to flash through key concepts, definitions and mnemonics. This will bring the points to the front of your short-term memory. You can capitalise on this (the Recency Principle of Memory) when you are inside the examination room. When you get inside the examination room write down as much as you can remember. You may be able to use this information during the examination. However, do not attempt to bring cue cards into the exam room with you.

Arrive at the examination hall in plenty of time.

It is inadvisable to discuss examination subject-related topics with colleagues beforehand or during the progress of the examinations at lunch break. This may cause confusion of ideas and any anxiety and lack of confidence they may have may be transmitted to you. Keep your brain crystal clear to maximise your concentration powers in the examination room.

Examination day

In the examination room when you receive the paper make sure that you read it from beginning to end. Before this, provided you have the opportunity while the invigilator is handing out the papers, write in your examination number on as many of the sheets of stationery provided as possible. This saves vital minutes later on and gets you a little bit more organised for the task ahead.

Read the instructions to candidates carefully. Decide what each question requires. Organise the order of the answers. Answer your 'best' question first, making sure you do not spend too long on it in relation to the marks available. Then tackle your 'second-best' question and so on. Remember you need not answer the questions in the numerical sequence given on the question paper itself. However, when finished you must put them in numerical sequence before you hand them in.

Your examination paper may contain a mix of long and short questions. Don't fall into the trap of assuming that length correlates with difficulty and thus avoid doing the long questions. In fact the converse is often true.

Answer the question asked and not some figment of your imagination. You must demonstrate a sufficient breadth and depth of knowledge as well as understanding to pass third-level examinations. You cannot do this adequately if you repeat the same information in different answers even if the questions given appear somewhat similar.

Budget your time

Budget your time carefully and stick to your time management plan. Do not ignore whole sections or spend too much time on one small section. Allocate time to each question in proportion to the marks given. Not answering all the questions/sections required shows the examiner that you have not covered the syllabus adequately, that you were banking on certain parts of the syllabus coming up or that you did not allocate your time properly in the examination room. Leave ten to fifteen minutes at the end of the paper for review and checking.

Candidates who take a chance and confine their study to a restricted area of the syllabus will almost certainly fail in any degree or professional examination.

When answering questions *concentrate on the main issue*. Do not be afraid to display as much relevant knowledge as possible. Support your points with relevant examples from your work experience. This is a very effective way of demonstrating knowledge and in professional examinations is one of the things the examiner is looking for. Theory is not much use if it can't be related to practice. One example to support each point is sufficient.

Plan your answers

In practice it has been found that most students tear into their answers and write straightaway. *Plan your answers for better presentation and more marks*. Make an outline Mind Map of the main ideas in your answer. Most examination questions are looking for answers with seven or eight points. Structure your paragraphs around these points. Use headings, subheadings and indentations to clarify your answers. Number and underline the headings for emphasis. A well laid out answer will make the examiner's job easier and win you extra marks at the same time.

For questions requiring a discussion, have an introduction, a middle (development of the theme) and a proper conclusion. Introductions should be short. It is better to get to the core of the question quickly. Sometimes a good diagram properly explained is the best way to answer an examination question (a picture speaks more than a thousand words). However, do not waste time by duplicating the information by words if the diagram is self-explanatory.

Adopt useful *time-saving devices* such as using initials or standard abbreviations of the subject providing you have explained the term or terms fully when introduced.

Write simply and to the point. Watch the following: grammar, spelling, punctuation, handwriting, paragraphing, layout and neatness. From an examiner's point of view there is nothing worse than script which looks like Chinese when it is meant to be English. The examiner is not going to waste valuable time trying to decipher the hieroglyphics. It is better to write less in an answer but legibly, rather than to write quickly and illegibly. So write clearly. Failure to do so will lose you marks as the examiner cannot award marks for something that cannot be read. And finally, if you have finished early do not leave the examination room. Stay and check your answers until the time allowed is up.

Advantages of planning

If you do not plan, your answer will present the examiner with pages of unrelieved and homogeneous script rather than proper paragraphed material. Also during the answer do not rephrase the facts of the problem stated in the question. This is a complete waste of precious examination time. Without planning you are more likely to wander all over the place and repeat points already made. Repetition using different phraseology does not fool the examiner.

Another advantage of planning your answers instead of writing non-stop for three hours is association. Ideas will often come to mind when planning the answer to one question which will help in answering another. However, don't rely on your memory, jot down the ideas as they come to mind. Your answers will more than reward the little effort and planning time expended. After all, the examiner has built a thinking time allowance into questions. Therefore, you are expected to think and reflect about the issues raised in the question. You cannot do this if you are writing all the time.

Planning will prevent you from attempting questions for which you have insufficient knowledge.

Thus, time wasting, panic reaction, switching to and fro between questions will be avoided. During the answering of questions you will also be less likely to become confused if working to a plan.

Causes of failure

For the average intelligent student the causes of failure have been identified as:

- Inadequate motivation and poor concentration (the approach to study).
- Bad study technique (studying itself).
- Poor examination technique (exhibiting the results of study).

It has been observed that success in most exams depends on a combination of:

- Inherent intelligence and special abilities;
- Effective study and examination techniques;
- Chance – the topics you have studied, or are good at, might just come up on the day!

Therefore, the chances of success are significantly greater for those who have been exposed to, and practised, proper study and examination techniques than for those who haven't. Finally, remember there is no substitute for hard work. Study techniques will only make the road a little easier; they won't get you through the examination on their own. You need an excellent grasp of the subject matter to pass the relevant papers. Genius has been defined as 1 per cent inspiration 99 per cent perspiration. So don't rely too much on your inspiration when examination time comes along!

Why examiners fail candidates

The following are summarised highlights of why examiners fail candidates. A little time invested by students reading a few examiners' reports should pay handsome dividends. After each cause of failure some tips are given on how the problem can be overcome.

Preparation. Many students are totally unprepared for the examination. Examining bodies are dedicated to maintaining high standards. Many business students, particularly those studying professional rather than degree courses, both work and pursue part-time studies. Consequently, you won't have as much time for study as say the average full-time arts student who generally has 15 hours in class each week and studies about 25 hours giving a total of 40 hours devoted to academic work. You spend anything up to 40 hours or more at work and need to clock in at least another 20 hours in private study and classroom work. Student's performance in examinations is directly correlated with the amount of time, application and effort put in. If you follow our advice your study time will be both productive and effective.

Presentation. Examiners often state that presentation is slovenly or of a standard quite unbecoming to an aspiring professional or graduate. Develop good presentation skills. Study the layout of suggested answers. In your working life slovenly work is likely to be returned to you for correction, modification or improvement. Similarly such work in examinations is unacceptable.

Answer the question set. The questions answered by candidates are sometimes unrelated to what is printed on the question papers. Read the questions carefully. *Pay particular attention to the 'requirement' section.* Realise that every word is important and means what it says and that extreme care has been taken by the examiners to ensure clarity. Look for key or limiting words. Use these to set the scope and limits of the question. Use the questioning technique. What is the question about? What does the examiner exactly want to know? Decide on the broad idea of the subject matter the question deals with. Then converge on the particular aspects that are required. Make sure your answer is relevant to the question as a whole. As you write the answer stop occasionally and check that your answer is consistently relevant to the question asked. This self-monitoring will prevent you straying away from the point.

Time management. The ability to work within time limits is an important element of a manager's work. It is also an important aspect of university degree and professional examinations. Poor usage of time in the examination hall has resulted in question papers not being finished in the time allowed. Allocate your time in proportion to the marks given. For a three hour paper this works out at 1.8 minutes per mark. So for a question with 30 marks you should allocate 54 minutes (1.8 × 30). Five minutes of this time should be reserved for planning and a few minutes should be set aside for review. Spend approximately 46 minutes actually doing the question. Apply the same approach to each question. Reserve a few minutes at the end of your examination to quickly review your entire script. Only add things at the end if, as you reread, you see that important conclusions are missing. If you run out of time and there is still one question unanswered, you could very well get some marks by outlining briefly how you would have answered the question.

A *law of diminishing returns* operates in relation to examination answers. The first 50 per cent of the marks for any question are much easier to get than the last 50 per cent. Similarly, the first few marks on a question are relatively easy to get, whereas the last few are extremely difficult to earn. Thus it is easier to score a few marks on a question which at first sight you thought you knew little about than spending more time on a question that you know a lot about and have already done justice to.

Balanced answers. You should write approximately the same length of answer to each question. For example, writing four pages of script for one question as against one for another shows either poor time management or a detailed knowledge of one topic and a superficial knowledge of another. Similarly, an unbalanced answer in which some sections receive too much attention shows a lack of planning or judgement and an inefficient use of time.

Write something. If you write nothing you cannot gain marks. Candidates who write something relevant will usually gain some marks. These marks could turn a borderline fail into a pass. Go into the examination determined to succeed. So give every question your best shot even if you feel you know very little about the topic.

Breadth of knowledge. Remember that examiners are looking for a breadth of knowledge over the whole syllabus, not depth of knowledge in a narrow field. So spending too much time on a favoured topic at the expense of others may cost you a pass. Time is also wasted by doing rough answers and then re-copying them.

Keep up to date. Many students are unaware of recent, relevant legislation, which results in outdated answers or outmoded layouts. Therefore, make sure that your textbooks are the most recent editions and that your notes are current. Purchasing secondhand books, while saving you money in the short term, could prove a poor investment in the long term. Also watch the financial press, business magazines, accountancy press and, in particular for accountancy students, accounting and student journals for new developments.

Multiple-choice questions

In a multiple-choice examination the student is required to select the correct or best response from several options. Items consist of a stem in the form of an incomplete statement, diagram, question, calculation or task to be solved. You must pick the correct response (called the key) from the options given. The incorrect responses are called distractors.

There are two basic kinds of multiple-choice questions. In one an incomplete statement can be combined with various options to make a complete statement which is either true or false. In the other a question is followed by various statements one of which must be chosen as the correct answer.

Objective testing is now a popular form of examination. Answers are either right or wrong. Multiple-choice questions are the most popular form of objective test. It is now used for some examination papers. The following approach to answering multiple-choice questions is suggested:

1. Read and heed the instructions. How much time is allowed? How exactly are you told to complete the answers? The latter is essential if the tests are computer scored.

2. Work through the whole paper. Answer those you find easy now. You can return to the more difficult questions later. Mark these on the margin with a question mark.

3. Highlight key words to ensure that you read and understand them fully.

4. Pick your best alternative, that is the one you feel is nearest the correct answer. Eliminate those you feel are incorrect. This will limit your choice and at the same time increase your chance of getting the right answer.

5. Don't procrastinate. You need to get through the test within the time constraints set. Time management is, therefore, of the utmost importance.

6. Return to the more difficult questions. On rereading, the answer may come to mind. Where you don't know the answer use logic and common sense. Random guesses are seldom correct.

Four basic ingredients for success

In the Report of the Examiners of a major professional body certain basic ingredients for success (equally applicable to any course of studies) in the examinations are recommended to candidates:

1. Follow an appropriate course of study.

2. Practise answering past questions and be fully aware of the rubric to each paper.

3. Get your tutor to criticise your work during practice sessions since only feedback of this nature can help you monitor your progress and remedy your shortcomings.

4. Plan your approach to the answering of the questions. Enter the examination hall not only armed with full knowledge but prepared to make full use of every moment of examination time. If only three-quarters of a paper is completed, then only three-quarters of that paper's marks are available.

With regard to point 2, students should be aware that for some professional exams, booklets of suggested answers are written by members of the examining panel. Students should study these to try to gauge the examiner's philosophy and see exactly the type of presentation, style, standard, content and emphasis the examiner expects. These are not normally published for university degree programmes. However, undergraduates might benefit by studying the equivalent subjects published by the professional bodies.

Examiners are human

Examiners are not ogres. They want you to pass the examination, but not at the expense of diluting standards. They have taken the examination themselves so they do empathise with you. However, do not write notes pleading to the examiner for leniency. This is both irritating to the examiner and a waste of your time.

Just like you, they get annoyed, irritated and bored. Marking papers can be a tedious job at the best of times. The examiner tries to mark them in a conscientious, fair and honourable fashion. To keep the examiner satisfied, interested and favourably disposed toward you, you should at least follow the rubric instructions and write legibly. If the examiner can't read what you have written then he can't award the appropriate marks.

Examiners know their subject, they can't be bluffed and they understand English. They are not interested in your pet theories, prejudices, religious beliefs, political opinions, moral judgements, social comment, biases, hatreds and so on. All they want is pertinent knowledge, facts and theory related to the question set. They take the most rational, sensible and logical interpretation of the questions set and mark accordingly. Great care is taken in formulating questions and they are checked and rechecked to ensure clarity and precision of words.

To pass you must reach a good standard in each paper as well as achieving a good overall standard. Some professional exam bodies publish explanation grades and band of marks covered by each. These are well worth consulting.

Systematic approach to answering questions

Develop the habit of going about answering questions in a mentally disciplined way. The following general approach (RTQPARM) is suggested.

Read the question. Concentrate on what you are required to do first as indicated at the end of the question. Then read all of the question a few times until you have the gist of what is required. Note any special requirements, such as list, detail, advise, explain, report and so on. When asked to list or outline do not give an essay. When asked to summarise do not give examples. When asked to report on, a report format is required. Failure to follow examination instructions will lose you marks. Please refer to the appendix for a glossary of terms used in examinations.

Think about the question. Think and reflect on the issues raised for a few moments. Stop and think should be your motto.

Question   What does the examiner want?
What is the subject area generally concerned with?
What are the fundamental issues behind the question?
What are the facts pertinent to the issues raised?
How can I present them in a clear, concise, lucid and logical fashion?

Plan. Draw a Mind Map of the key points to answer the question. Ask yourself again if these points are truly relevant to the question asked.

Answer. Use the key points of your plan as captions and write a paragraph around each. Stop after every few paragraphs and recheck that you are being consistently relevant and are not straying from the point. Use a Deductive approach (make an inference from general theories to the particular problem posed). This is in preference to an Inductive approach (where students try to draw general conclusions from specific examples or, indeed, personal views).

Remember: examinations are tests of theoretical knowledge.

Theory may be illustrated by practical relevant experience. This is recommended, as it shows that the candidate can relate theory to practice. However, inventing your own theories, which is what you are actually doing by drawing general inferences from your own practical experience or personal views, is not acceptable to examiners. The examiner requires evidence in the form of well balanced arguments supported by reference to authors, books, articles, research studies and also radio and television documentaries.

Review. Quickly review your answer, picking up misspellings, incomplete or nonsensical statements, lack of conclusions and so on. Apply logic to calculations. Check that they are within the parameters of the 'ball park,' figures which you should have precalculated on a commonsense basis for comparison as to reasonableness.

Move. Move on the the next question and start the RTQPARM approach again.

Summary

You should have a systematic examination revision plan in operation during the last two weeks. Get past examination questions with model answers and work through them. Make sure you master frequently recurring topics.

In the examination room read right through the examination paper and make sure you read both sides of the sheet so that you see all of the questions. Allocate time to each question in proportion to the marks given and spend about five minutes planning your answer before attempting the question. Make sure you undertake all the required questions.

Apart from lack of inherent intelligence the reasons why people fail examinations are lack of proper motivation, poor study, and sloppy examination technique.

The following are some of the basic reasons why candidates fail examinations.

- Inadequate preparation.

- Poor presentation.

- Failure to answer the question set.

- Bad time management.

- Failure to keep up to date.

    A suggested approach to multiple choice questions was outlined.

    The four basic ingredients for success are:

- Follow an appropriate course of study.

- Practise answering past papers.

- Get feedback from your tutor.

- Plan your answers.

    Remember, examiners are human. However, they do need your co-operation to help them get you through the examinations. So watch your layout and follow the rubric.

    Use a systematic approach to answering questions as follows.

- **R**ead the question carefully.

- **T**hink about the question.

- **Q**uestion the question.

- **P**lan your answer.

- **A**nswer the question.

- **R**eview your answer.

- **M**ove on to the next question.

GOOD LUCK IN YOUR EXAMINATIONS! YOU CAN DO IT!

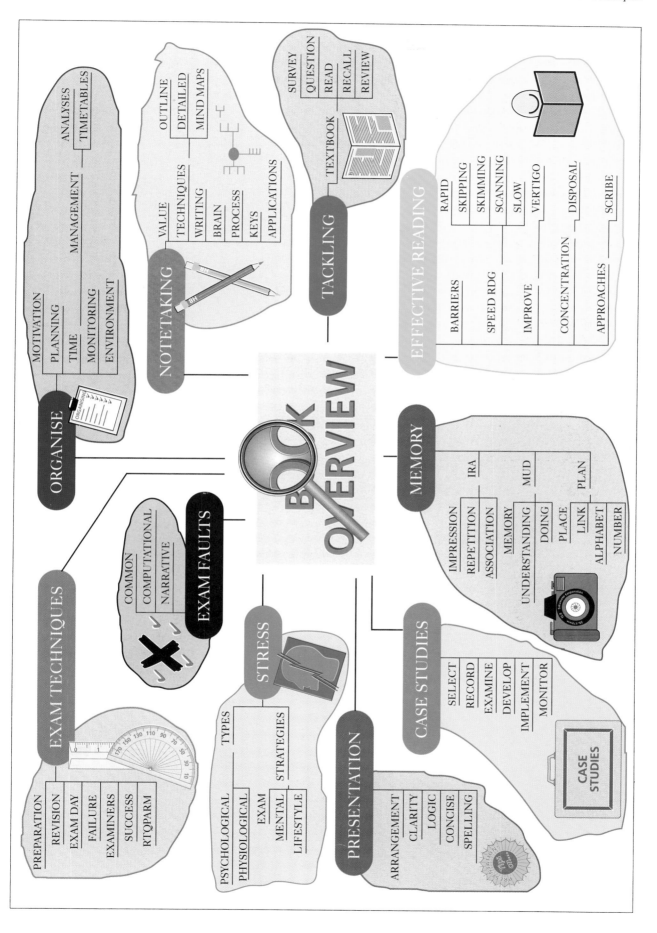

BOOK OVERVIEW

ORGANISE
- MOTIVATION
- PLANNING
- TIME
- MONITORING
- ENVIRONMENT
- MANAGEMENT
  - ANALYSES
  - TIMETABLES

ORGANISING

NOTETAKING
- VALUE
- TECHNIQUES
- WRITING
- BRAIN
- PROCESS
- KEYS
- APPLICATIONS
  - OUTLINE
  - DETAILED
  - MIND MAPS

HB

TACKLING
- TEXTBOOK
  - SURVEY
  - QUESTION
  - READ
  - RECALL
  - REVIEW

EFFECTIVE READING
- RAPID
  - SKIPPING
  - SKIMMING
  - SCANNING
  - SLOW
  - VERTIGO
- BARRIERS
- SPEED RDG
- IMPROVE
  - CONCENTRATION
    - DISPOSAL
    - SCRIBE
  - APPROACHES

MEMORY
- IMPRESSION
- REPETITION
- ASSOCIATION
- MEMORY
- UNDERSTANDING
  - IRA
  - MUD
    - DOING
    - PLACE
    - LINK
    - ALPHABET
    - NUMBER
    - PLAN

EXAM TECHNIQUES
- PREPARATION
- REVISION
- EXAM DAY
- FAILURE
- EXAMINERS
- SUCCESS
- RTQPARM

EXAM FAULTS
- COMMON
- COMPUTATIONAL
- NARRATIVE

STRESS
- TYPES
- STRATEGIES
- PSYCHOLOGICAL
- PHYSIOLOGICAL
- EXAM
- MENTAL
- LIFESTYLE

PRESENTATION
- ARRANGEMENT
- CLARITY
- LOGIC
- CONCISE
- SPELLING

PRESENTATION

CASE STUDIES
- SELECT
- RECORD
- EXAMINE
- DEVELOP
- IMPLEMENT
- MONITOR

CASE STUDIES

Appendix
Glossary of Terms Frequently Used in Examination Questions

Advise/recommend	Present information, opinions or recommendations to someone to enable the recipient to take action.
Amplify	Expand or enlarge upon the meaning of (a statement or quotation).
Analyse	Determine and explain the constituent parts of.
Appraise/assess/evaluate	Judge the importance or value of.
Assess	See 'appraise'.
Clarify	Explain more clearly the meaning of.
Comment (critically)	Explain.
Compare (with)	Explain similarities and differences between.
Contrast	Place in opposition to bring out difference(s).
Criticise	Present the faults in a theory or policy or opinion.
Demonstrate	Show by reasoning the truth of.
Describe	Present the details and characteristics of.
Discuss	Explain the opposing arguments.
Distinguish	Specify the difference between.
Evaluate	See 'appraise'.
Explain/interpret	Set out in detail the meaning of.
Illustrate	Use an example – chart, diagram, graph or figure as appropriate – to explain something.
Interpret	See 'explain'.
Justify	State adequate grounds for.
List (and explain)	Itemise (and detail the meaning of).
Prove	Show by testing the accuracy of.
Recommend	See 'advise'.
Reconcile	Make compatible apparently conflicting statements or theories.
Relate	Show connections between separate matters.
State	Express.
Summarise	State briefly the essential points (dispensing with examples and details).
Tabulate	Set out facts or figures in a table.

References and Bibliography

Acres, D. 1988. *How to Pass Exams without Anxiety*. Northcote House Publishers

Allen, Clifford. 1972. *Passing Examinations*. Pan Books

Buzan, Tony. 1974. *Use Your Head*. BBC Publications

Buzan, Tony. 1993. *The Mind Map Book*. BBC Publications

Davis, D. 1986. *Maximising Examination Performance, A Psychological Approach*. Kogan Page

Easton, G. 1983. *Learning from Case Studies*. Prentice-Hall

Gagne, Robert M. 1977. *The Conditions of Learning*. Holt-Saunders International

Hanson, P. 1988. *The Joy of Stress*. Pan Books

Kellett, Michael. 1980. *Memory Power*. Sterling Publishing

Lorayne, Harry, and Lucas, Jerry. 1976. *The Memory Book*. Starr Books

Maddox, H. 1967. *How to Study*. Pan Books

Malone, S A. 1992. *Better Exam Results*. CIMA

Malone, S A. 1995. *A Critical Evaluation of Mind Maps in an Adult Learning Environment*. Dissertation submitted for M.Ed degree of the University of Sheffield

Norfolk, D. 1987. *Executive Stress*. Arrow Books

Shone, R. 1984. *Creative Visualisation*. Thorsons

Rowntree, Derek. 1970. *Learn How to Study*. McDonald

Russell, Peter. 1979. *The Brain Book*. Routledge and Kegan Paul

Wingfield. 1979. *Human Learning and Memory*. Harper and Row